LEBNANI

*A journey through family, food
and the flavours of Lebanon*

Jad Youssef

Meze Publishing Limited

1b, 2 Kelham Square

Sheffield

S3 8SD

First published in Great Britain by Meze Publishing

Photographs © Matt Russell

Copyright Text © Jad Youssef

Jad Youssef asserts their moral right to be identified as the author of this work.

ISBN 978-1-915538-45-1

A CIP catalogue record for this book is available from the British Library.

Photography: Matt Russell

Art Director & Props Stylist: Tabitha Hawkins

Editor: Katie Fisher

Creative Lead: Patrick Budge

Design: Paul Cocker

Food Stylist: Eleanor Mulligan

Assistant Food Stylist: Jad Youssef

Contents

Introduction 5

Our Dishes 14

Lebanese Mornings 22

Mezza at Home 44

Classic Mezza 78

Tabkha 108

Mashawi 142

Sandwiché 160

Hélweyét 178

Namlieh 192

Glossary 207

Index 208

Acknowledgements 216

The people and food of Lebanon

The story behind Lebnani

Marhaba,

Before we step into the recipes, and before we begin cooking together, I want to tell you a little about where I come from, about Lebanon, and why this book exists. This is not just a cookbook – this is my story, my family's story, and, in many ways, the story of Lebanon itself.

I grew up in Beirut during the 1970s and '80s, a city vibrant with life but scarred by conflict. I was born just two years after the civil war shattered Lebanon's peace, and so my entire childhood unfolded against the backdrop of a country at war. For over fifteen years, conflict coloured everything: our home, education, friendships, and family life. There were times when school was interrupted for weeks or months, when we had to leave our home for safer towns and villages. Sirens, gunfire, roadblocks – these were part of our everyday landscape. Life in Beirut was complicated, but even in the shadow of war, something stronger always pulled us together: family and food.

Despite falling bombs and regular power cuts, the question in our home every morning remained the same: 'What shall we eat today?' Food was our way of creating normality, of keeping family close, of finding joy. This is something deeply rooted in Lebanese culture – no matter what happens, we gather, we cook, and we eat together. Whatever what was taking place outside our door, the kitchen remained our sanctuary. It was where life felt normal, even beautiful. Amid all the uncertainty, the rhythm of cooking and eating gave our days structure and comfort. This pattern of gathering, cooking, eating, and sharing is deeply woven into the Lebanese identity. It has carried us through generations, through war, through peace, always bringing us back to the table.

My family's story, like so many Lebanese stories, begins in the South – the rural, fertile heart of the country. It is a land of ancient olive trees, groves of figs and pomegranates, hillsides dotted with za'atar and sumac. The air carries the scent of the earth itself: sun-dried herbs, ripening fruit, and the breeze from nearby rivers and lakes. These southern lands

With Mum and Dad, early 1980s –
Mum's kibbé and that homely smell
I'll never forget.

are not only the foundation of our food and culture; they are also the heartbeat of our traditions.

Even today, my family still picks and presses its own olives there. That olive oil flows into our kitchens and into our hearts – it's part of who we are. In Lebanon, if your family doesn't own olive trees, you turn to your friends, your neighbours, your community, and you share. The land feeds not just our bodies, but our relationships. In many ways, every drop of olive oil carries the taste of family and friendship.

My father, like so many others in the 1960s and '70s, left the South for Beirut, seeking safety and opportunity. But my grandparents and aunts remained, tending to the land, preserving the old ways that flavour our food to this day. I can still see my mother and aunt climbing into the mountains, gathering wild za'atar and sumac, spreading them out to dry on the rooftops under the sun. Later, they would gently crush the dried herbs by hand, filling our home with that unmistakable southern scent. Even now, opening a jar of za'atar in my kitchen takes me straight back to those long, warm summer afternoons.

Food in Lebanon isn't simply something we consume. It shapes our days, our seasons, our entire way of living. Deciding on your next meal is a daily ritual that brings the whole family together, in discussion, in planning, in joyful anticipation. My mother would wake us in the morning with a gentle smile, and before anything else, she would ask what we wanted for breakfast, for lunch, for dinner. That conversation never ended – it would flow through the entire day, always circling back to the meals we would share.

Even the simplest dishes involve the whole family. Everyone has a voice; everyone is part of the preparation. A humble bowl of lentil and Swiss chard soup, a fresh fattoush, fasoulia (butter bean and lamb stew), stuffed courgettes, slow-cooked green beans with tomatoes… each dish is prepared with the same care and love, no matter how ordinary it may seem. To say that Lebanese people are obsessed with food is true, but it's not about indulgence. It's about gratitude, connection, and honouring those who came before us.

And the act of cooking itself was never just about the food; it was about the people we cooked for. Every dish carried memories, stories, and, often, silent acts of love. Preparing food for family and friends is one of the purest ways we express care for each other. Sitting around the table together was our time to share stories, laughter, and sometimes even tears. The table was where we reconnected at the end of every day.

Lebanese cooking is not complicated, but it is deeply intentional. We believe in the purity of ingredients, in freshness, in letting the land speak through its flavours. Even now, as I cook in my restaurant and at home, I carry that same passion I learned as a boy – the joy of simplicity, balance, patience.

Shopping for food is also its own sacred ritual. In Lebanon, we don't fill trolleys once a week. We rise early and head to the souks and markets, where farmers arrive at dawn with their harvest, fishermen display the night's catch, butchers prepare fresh lamb and veal each morning. The produce is seasonal, local, honest – you buy what the land gives you. By noon, most of the shopping is done, the freshest ingredients already in kitchens, ready to be transformed into the day's meals.

Some of my family were butchers. Others were bakers. Often, they worked side by side, doors open to the warm breeze, the scents of baking bread and grilled meats mingling. As the youngest of six siblings, I had my role too. Each morning, my mother would prepare a tray carefully arranged with halloumi cheese, olive oil, and za'atar. My job was to carry that tray to the local baker. He would roll out the dough, shape the edges, build the mana'eesh, our beloved flatbread, and slide it into the wood-fired oven. I would stand there, breathing in the scent of burning wood, watching the bread rise and blister, then carefully carry the hot, fragrant loaves home for breakfast.

At the time, I may have seen it as a chore. But now I understand that those simple routines gifted me something precious, a quiet education in the rhythm, care, and intimacy of Lebanese food. They taught me patience, pride, and the joy of feeding others. And my learning didn't stop there. As I grew older, I spent more time helping my parents with the work that surrounded food. I would walk with my mother to the market stalls, learning how to feel for the best tomatoes, what the freshest herbs smelled like, how to judge each ingredient by sight, touch, and smell. These were not just lessons in shopping, they were lessons in respect for the food we would bring to our table.

Often, I would also join my father on his rounds to buy supplies for his pastry shop. He didn't drive, so we would walk to the shops together – the grocery store was just one street away in the neighbouring district,

With Dad and my sisters,
his arghileh always nearby.

but with heavy bags in hand, it often felt like a long journey for my small arms. We carried the bags in rounds, splitting the weight between us. Sometimes, I felt like the bags were heavier than me. But at the end of the day, my father always had a sweet reward waiting for me: a slice of his semolina cake, soft and sticky with dates. To this day, I can still taste that treat after those long walks.

These are small memories, but they shaped everything. My understanding of food, of family, of work, of life itself, was all learned without words, simply by being present.

Lebanon is a small country – you can cross it north to south in just a few hours – but within its borders lies a world rich in history, culture, beauty, and, sadly, conflict. To the north and east lies Syria; to the south, Palestine; to the west, the Mediterranean Sea. Sometimes, you can stand at Lebanon's edge and still hear the distant echoes of war. But when you turn towards its heart, you find something else entirely: resilience, hospitality, and lives built around family, community, and food.

What it means to be Lebnani

To be Lebnani is to be Lebanese. It means being part of a culture that finds strength in family, comfort in tradition, and joy in every meal. The restaurant we built in Reigate carries that spirit. And now, so does this book.

I want to take you beyond the headlines you may have read about Lebanon. Yes, my country has known war, but it has also known great beauty, warmth, and resilience. Through the recipes of my mother, my aunts, and my grandparents, I want you to experience the Lebanon I know – humble, generous, and full of life.

This book is not simply a collection of recipes. It is my attempt to bring you into my Lebanon, to sit you at my family's table, to share our stories, to pass on the traditions, and to cook as we cook. The recipes here are not modernised or adapted for Western trends. You won't find hummus with beetroot, fattoush with sweet potato, baked falafel, or cauliflower shawarma. You will find the recipes I grew up with, as they were taught to me by members of my family – dishes prepared for generations in our kitchens. Simple. Honest. Delicious. Food that reflects the soul of Lebanon.

Because Lebanese food is not only about flavour. It's about where that flavour comes from: the olives picked by hand, the za'atar dried beneath the sun, the bread baked at dawn, the souks buzzing with life, the families gathered around tables, sharing stories as generously as they share plates.

A visual journey

While working on this book, I had hoped to return again to the South, to the Békaa Valley, to sit with my family and capture for you the real life of Lebanon. But the country's instability made that impossible, at least for now. Still, through these words and recipes I hope you will feel the Lebanon I carry within me. The Lebanon that shaped me. The Lebanon I am proud to share with you.

Throughout these pages, you will also see Lebanon as I see it, in photographs old and new, from vintage images of Beirut to the kitchens where my family still cooks. You'll see the bustling markets, the olive groves, the pomegranate trees, and the tables full of mezza where every meal is a celebration.

This is my Lebanon. This is my family. This is my passion.
And now, it is my privilege to share it with you.

Yalla. Let's cook.

Our Dishes

I wanted to share some of the core memories that surround several of Lebanon's most iconic dishes for me – from mana'eesh in the mornings and sizzling lahém b'ajine on southern road trips to how we really make tabbouleh, hummus, and falafel. There are plenty more stories throughout the recipes that follow, but these dishes deserve a moment in the spotlight and I hope they help to welcome you into my Lebanon.

Mana'eesh Jibneh – the morning that belongs to everyone

Mana'eesh jibneh wasn't just something we ate for breakfast; it was how the day began. In our house, it was almost sacred. My mum would start early, quietly, before the rest of the family stirred. She'd soak the Akkawi cheese to soften its saltiness, gently shred it with her hands, and mix it with some Nabulsi cheese to give the right pull and softness when baked. She'd drizzle over a little olive oil, just enough to bring everything together, and then place it in a round metal tray.

That tray was my job. My task was to carry it, carefully balanced, covered in a tea towel, to a bakery not even in our own neighbourhood. When I'd ask why we couldn't use the closer one, my mother would say 'because their oven doesn't talk to the dough'. That's how it was: poetic, stubborn, and absolutely right. So I'd walk, often reluctantly, through the sleepy streets, holding that tray of cheese like it was gold. Truth is, I never liked that walk. I always felt exposed, a boy cutting through alleys and across corners while people stared or smiled. But something changed when I reached the bakery. The moment I stepped inside, I was part of something bigger.

On Sunday mornings especially, the place was alive. Loud, smoky, busy, a beautiful kind of chaos. The scent of toasted za'atar, the puff of rising dough, the heat of the oven pouring into the room. There were people elbowing their way to the front, old men leaning against the wall chatting about politics, kids like me holding trays from their mothers, teenagers eating mana'eesh fresh from the oven, standing outside and licking their fingers between bites. Some came for the ready-made ones, others like me came with their own cheese. No matter where you were from or who you were, you waited your turn. You became part of the rhythm.

The baker, with his apron covered in flour and his arms moving like he was dancing with the fire, would glance up and nod. He knew. He already had rounds of dough flattened on wooden boards waiting for toppings. He'd hand me one, and I'd spread the cheese myself – edge to edge, not too thick – and pass it back. In minutes, it would slide into the hot, deep oven to emerge golden and bubbling, folded gently, steam rising in the air. The baker would stack them back on my tray, one by one, the aroma like something holy.

I'd walk home slower. The streets felt different with that warm scent floating up from under the cloth. And when I reached the door, Mum would lift the towel, smile, and call everyone to the table. We'd eat them with tomatoes, olives, maybe some fresh mint, torn with our hands and enjoyed with stories from the night before.

This same scene plays out across every city, town, and village in Lebanon. From the narrow streets of Beirut to the hills of Aley, from the coastal bakeries of Saida to the backyards of Nabatieh – mana'eesh jibneh is our shared language. Every mother sends her child to the best oven, every child knows the weight of that tray, and every neighbourhood has that one bakery where the dough is just right. The shouting, the laughing, the aromas, they are the morning music of Lebanon.

Mana'eesh is not just food. It's habit. It's memory. It's identity. It's knowing that somewhere out there, someone else is spreading cheese on dough just like you, waiting for the heat to turn it into something comforting and familiar. That's what mana'eesh means to me. Not just a recipe, but a ritual that belongs to all of us.

Mana'eesh Za'atar – the land in your hands

There's a reason mana'eesh za'atar smells like Lebanon in the morning. Not just because it's everywhere in Beirut's side-street bakeries, or on a mountain breakfast table, but because of the story behind it, and how deeply rooted it is in our soil.

Za'atar, in the South, is more than a herb. It's a ritual. The wild kind, za'atar barri, grows along hillsides, stone walls, and red clay roads. It's picked during the heat of late spring or early summer, just before it flowers fully. My mother used to say, 'when the scent hits your nose before your hand touches the bush, it's ready'. We'd go out with baskets before sunrise, to avoid the scorching heat. The women – my mum, aunties and sometimes even Teta, my grandmother – would gently pinch the sprigs by hand, never pulling too hard. Wild za'atar doesn't like greed. They'd gather only what they needed, leaving roots and enough leaves for next season. It's a kind of respect that only farmers and foragers understand.

Back home, the za'atar was laid out on clean white sheets atop the balcony or rooftop to dry – turning it every few hours, brushing away dust, removing sticks and stones. Once dry, it was rubbed and crushed by hand in large shallow trays. The smell of crushed za'atar would fill the whole house: earthy, lemony, slightly bitter.

Then came the mixing. Every family had their own téh'wijé (blend). In the South, our blend always had more thyme than in the North; we'd go with about six parts dried za'atar leaves, two parts roasted sesame seeds, and one to two parts crushed sumac depending on the acidity of that year's batch. A little salt, and that's it. And when Mum would mix it with extra virgin olive oil – real, green, bold southern oil – it turned into a paste that felt alive. Thick but pourable, sharp but rounded. She'd spoon it into a bowl and hand it to me. 'Spread it properly, not too thin, not too thick.' I'd take it with the dough tray to the bakery. The oil would drip on my fingers as I walked. I'd complain, but deep down, I loved that walk.

Like mana'eesh jibneh, mana'eesh za'atar is more than just breakfast. It's the land in your hands. It's your family. It's your Lebanon.

Lahém b'Ajine – the taste of travelling south

These flatbreads don't just remind me of the kitchen, they remind me of the road, the scent of pine trees, the hum of the car engine heading south. Whenever we were travelling to the South, often in summer or on a family weekend, there was always one sacred stop along the way: Abu Abbas. A small, slightly hidden butcher-bakery, known to locals but loved deeply by us. He was my father's cousin, and they would greet each other with a handshake that lasted a full conversation.

I remember my dad standing in the middle of the tiled butcher's shop, pointing at cuts, arguing gently about which part to use for the lahém b'ajine. He always asked for the shoulder – lean yet tender, with just enough fat to make the topping juicy. The butcher would nod, disappear to the back, and reappear with a tray of freshly minced lamb, ground just for us. Then it was off to the baker next door, shouting out orders and arranging the rounds of dough on wide wooden boards. We didn't get a few. We got dozens of those small lahém b'ajine, each the size of a hand, bubbling hot, edges crisp, the meat fragrant with tomato and pomegranate molasses.

We'd carry the trays back to the car, the aroma filling every corner. And not five minutes later, we'd pull over into the first patch of forest off the main road, a shady spot with pine needles on the ground and the scent of the sea already in the breeze. That was our picnic. We'd open the boxes, burn our fingers a little, and pass them around. Everyone quiet, chewing, smiling. No plates, just fingers, lemons and napkins. That moment, those flatbreads, that quiet pine-covered roadside still feels like the beginning of any real road trip.

In every Lebanese town, whether in Saida, Nabatieh, or the Békaa, you'll find a version of this dish. Some make it fiery, others milder. But the soul remains the same: dough, meat, spice, and a memory tucked into each bite.

Khadija's Tabbouleh – a bowl full of home

My mother's tabbouleh was famous in the family. The care she gave it taught me more about cooking than any professional kitchen ever did. She would sit by the window with a large colander of parsley, not in a rush. Each bunch was picked by hand, leaf by leaf, any yellow or tough parts discarded. She'd spread the herbs on a clean towel to dry in the air, never using a spinner, never forcing the process. Mint was treated the same, picked fresh that morning. Her knife was always sharp, and I still remember the fine rhythmic sound it made on the board as she chopped. This, too, was never rushed and always done by hand, as this is what gives tabbouleh its signature lightness.

For my mother, the balance of flavours mattered most. 'It should taste of parsley first, not of bulgur,' she would say. In our home, we used very little bulgur, just enough to give body without overwhelming the herbs. Tomatoes were ripe and sweet, onions crisp, and the seasoning was always tasted and adjusted at the end. No measuring spoons – just the tongue and the memory of how it should taste. Lemon was never shy; olive oil was generous but never heavy.

When it came to serving, the tabbouleh was always presented in a large, wide bowl so everyone could reach in easily. We ate it with lettuce leaves, sometimes cabbage, and there were always olives on the side, sometimes radishes too. It was a dish to linger over, bite after bite, not a quick salad to finish. At big family gatherings, it was always refilled. No matter how many other dishes were on the table, the tabbouleh bowl would be scraped clean first.

Even today, whenever I make it, I can still hear my mother saying 'don't rush. Tabbouleh is made with the hands, not the clock.' And that is the truth of it in Lebanon – tabbouleh is not about technique, it's about respect, rhythm, and knowing when it tastes just right.

Hummus – simple, honest, ours

For us Lebanese, hummus is more than a recipe, it's a part of who we are. It's not a garnish or a filler on the table; it's a dish that commands space, presence, and respect. Every Lebanese, no matter how humble or grand their kitchen, knows how to make hummus. And not just make it, perfect it. The balance of tahini, the sharpness of lemon, the right texture – it's a skill passed down like a sacred rite, from mother to daughter, from father to son.

Historically, hummus runs deep. It dates back to the ancient Levant – Syria, Lebanon, Palestine – long before national borders, when food travelled with people, but roots were still strong. Lebanon embraced hummus early and completely. It found its place at the heart of the mezza – the traditional spread that brings everyone together. And in Lebanese homes, hummus was always made fresh. Soaking the chickpeas overnight. Using pure tahini. Pressing fresh lemon juice. It's a process that says: this is worth waiting for.

The bowl of hummus, placed in the middle of the mezza table, is not just a starter. It's the centrepiece. It invites sharing. It brings silence, then stories, then laughter. It doesn't ask for applause, it simply does its job, quietly nourishing the room with its smooth richness. We gather around it, tear bread, dip, talk. We never eat hummus alone.

But in recent years, that sacred bowl has been hijacked.

Outside Lebanon, hummus has exploded in popularity – but not in the right way. It's being blended, coloured, twisted. With beetroot. With chocolate. With pumpkin spice. With curry. Even with peanut butter. What was once a proud Levantine icon is now treated like a trend, a novelty, a blank canvas to be played with. But hummus is not merely a dip. It's not an appetiser. It's not meant to be squeezed into supermarket tubs with a week-long shelf life. Every addition of flavour takes it further from what it is and from who we are. These modern versions remove the memory from hummus. There's no soaking, no patience, no tasting and adjusting, no gathering. Just marketing. And slowly, all of this erases the quiet beauty of its simplicity.

For us, the beauty of hummus is in its purity. Chickpeas, cooked soft and sweet. Tahini, slightly bitter and deep. Lemon, sharp and bright. Garlic for punch. Salt for balance. And the olive oil – always Lebanese, always cold-pressed, flowing on top like a golden blessing. This is not just food. This is ours. A dish that connects us to generations before us. To our grandmothers, who would mash it in large mortars. To our parents, who showed us how to taste, adjust, respect. And to our children, who we hope will carry that same pride.

So yes, let others discover hummus. Let the world enjoy it. But let's not allow it to be redefined. Let it be known for what it truly is, not a flavour to be fused, but a culture to be preserved. And always, always eat it with warm Lebanese flatbread. Soft, tearable, humble. Not crackers or crisps. Just bread, the way it's been for centuries. That's how we protect the soul of our food. That's how we protect who we are.

Falafel – crispy on the outside, fluffy on the inside

In Lebanon, falafel belongs to the street. It is the food of the souk, of the old city, of small family-run shops passed down through generations. You smell it before you see it: the scent of herbs, spices, and frying oil drifting down the street. It stops you in your tracks. You follow it to a small doorway, sometimes no more than a counter, where a man in an apron is working the fryer, shaping falafel by hand or with a well-worn mould, dropping them into bubbling oil.

As a child, when my mother took me into Beirut, to Hamra or Tariq el-Jadida, the falafel shops were always part of the day. We would stop to eat, always standing, never sitting. No plates, no cutlery – just hot falafel, wrapped in thin flatbread, with crisp lettuce, parsley, tomatoes, pickles, and a generous spoonful of tarator. The man would hand it to you wrapped in paper, still hot, with oil soaking through. You ate it with your hands, tearing the bread and scooping up the filling as you went. It was noisy, fast, communal.

In my family, falafel was always bought from the street. My mother never made it at home, not because she couldn't, but because it was part of going out, part of the life of the city. And the falafel man was a master. He would start early in the morning, soaking chickpeas and fava overnight, grinding them fresh, letting the batter rest before the first batch hit the oil. By noon, you'd see the queue outside his shop.

Falafel is not a dish of the elite. It is the people's food: cheap, filling, full of flavour. Every shop has its own way – some use more chickpeas, others more fava. The spice blend is often a family secret. But one thing never changes: falafel is fried. In Lebanon, we don't serve falafel baked or made with other vegetables. That is not our way. Falafel is green and herbaceous inside, crisp and golden outside. When fried in good oil, with fresh herbs, it is light – never greasy. This is why people line up for it, not for gimmicks, but for the real thing.

Even today, after twenty-five years of cooking professionally, I still say falafel is not to be reinvented. It is a dish to be respected. Its beauty is in its simplicity – in the crunch of the outer shell, the softness inside, the balance of garlic, cumin, coriander, and fresh herbs. Served with hot bread, sharp pickles, and creamy tahini sauce, you don't need anything more. In this book, I give you the real falafel – the way it should be. Not modernised. Not changed. The Lebanon I grew up with, and the Lebanon I will pass on to my children.

Lebanese Mornings

Térwi'aa – the soulful start to a Lebanese day

In Lebanon, breakfast isn't just the first meal of the day – it's a ritual of comfort, flavour, and togetherness. We don't rush it with cereal or coffee on the go. We sit, we share, we scoop with warm bread, we talk. It's a spread, a table filled with small plates, colours, textures, and the aromas of olive oil, za'atar, labneh, freshly cut tomatoes, mint, cucumbers, and, of course, the essential olives. This is what we call térwi'aa – a word that carries more than just the idea of breakfast. It's how we fuel the day, the way we welcome the morning with presence and purpose.

Growing up, weekends meant gathering around the kitchen table with my parents and sisters, the windows wide open to the sound of the street – a neighbour sweeping her doorstep, the honk of a man delivering kaak, the clatter of plates, and kettles whistling. My mum would lay out the khobez, still warm from the bakery down the road, and we'd all dig in. One person would crush garlic into labneh, another would drizzle olive oil and sumac over tomatoes. Every person had their role. No eggs without mint. No mana'eesh without sweet black tea or a glass of cold laban.

And even when things were hard – during the war, or when money was tight – there was always breakfast. Simple but dignified. A boiled egg, a piece of cheese, and olives from the last season's harvest. Lebanese families know how to turn a few good ingredients into something beautiful, something that fills more than your stomach.

This chapter is a tribute to that breakfast table. To the mornings that shaped my love for food. To the memories of sitting on the cool kitchen tiles, dipping bread into labneh while the grownups argued about politics. To my dad, reading the newspaper with one hand and holding a slice of tomato with the other. To the feeling that no matter what the day would bring, you started it with love and food that was worth waking up for.

So, welcome to térwi'aa. This is how we begin.

Ful w Hummus
فول وحمص

Creamy fava beans & chickpeas mashed with garlic, lemon & olive oil: the king of breakfast

Serves 4–5

1 x 400g jar or tin of chickpeas (or see the recipe for hummus on page 80)

2 x 400g jars or tins of ful medammas (cooked fava beans)

4–5 garlic cloves, finely grated

1 tsp fine sea salt, or to taste

Juice of 2 lemons (approx. 80ml)

5–6 tbsp excellent extra virgin olive oil

To garnish and serve

10–15 fresh parsley leaves, chopped

Sprinkle of ground cumin (optional)

1 small vine tomato, diced

2 vine tomatoes, cut into wedges

3–4 radishes, sliced

3–4 whole spring onions

3–4 stalks of fresh mint

Warm Lebanese khobez

Green chillies and pickles (optional)

In every Lebanese home, even the most traditional ones, there are always ready-made jars of ful and hummus stashed in the pantry. Teta might soak the beans from scratch on Sundays, but during the week she'd grab a jar of good quality ful to warm up with garlic, lemon, and oil and just like that, breakfast was ready. So this version is not a shortcut – it's just as authentic as the slow one. What matters is the care in the seasoning, the quality of the olive oil, and how it's served. Many Lebanese actually prefer the jarred versions because the beans are soft, earthy, and consistent.

Rinse the chickpeas lightly if they come in salted water. Pour them into a saucepan along with the jars of ful and their liquid. Heat gently over medium-low heat until simmering. Using a wooden spoon, lightly mash some of the fava beans against the side of the pot – not fully, just to add texture.

Crush the garlic with the salt until creamy. Add the lemon juice and olive oil to the garlic, whisk into an emulsion, then adjust the salt and lemon to taste.

Once the ful w hummus is hot, turn off the heat. Spoon into wide, shallow bowls. Drizzle generously with the garlic and lemon dressing, then top with the chopped parsley, a sprinkle of cumin if desired, and the diced tomato. Serve alongside the vegetables and herbs, warm khobez (torn, not sliced), and the chillies and pickles if you like.

After a plate of ful w hummus, we sip hot black tea with fresh mint, often sweetened, served in small glasses. An arghileh follows for me. The kitchen is quickly wiped clean, Fairouz hums in the background, and the day begins — full, content, and grounded.

Beid w Banadoura
بيض وبندورة

*Lebanese-style eggs with fresh tomatoes
& olive oil*
Serves 4–5

5–6 ripe medium tomatoes (about 750g)

4 tbsp extra virgin olive oil

4 garlic cloves, finely minced

1 tsp fine sea salt, or to taste

¼ tsp freshly ground black pepper

1 tsp tomato paste (optional, for richer
colour and depth in winter)

6 large free-range eggs

Fresh mint or parsley, for garnish
(optional)

Beid w Banadoura wasn't just a breakfast dish, it was the
heart of any morning gathering in the house. My mother
would prepare it whenever we had fresh tomatoes from
the garden, and the aroma would travel across the house,
calling everyone in. In our village, that meant it was time
to stop what you were doing – whether you were out in the
field or sitting by the fire, it pulled you back to the table. I
remember the times when my father would rush in from the
orchard, just as the eggs were cracking into the bubbling
sauce, and he'd smile: 'No one does it like you, Khadija'.
There were never any leftovers – the tomatoes absorbed the
richness of the eggs, and the olive oil made everything feel
like it came from the earth itself. It was a dish of simplicity
and comfort.

Wash the tomatoes thoroughly in cold water. Score a small x on the
bottom of each and blanch in boiling water for 30 seconds. Transfer
to cold water, peel off the skins, and chop roughly.

In a wide sauté pan or sajiyyeh, heat the olive oil over medium heat.
Add the minced garlic and cook gently for 30 seconds until just
fragrant – don't let it brown. Add the tomatoes, salt, and pepper. Let
the mixture simmer for 10–12 minutes, stirring occasionally, until
it breaks down into a thick, saucy consistency. If the tomatoes are
very watery, cook a little longer. In winter, stir in the tomato paste for
richness.

Taste the sauce and adjust the seasoning, then make 6 small wells in
the sauce and crack in the eggs one by one. Cover the pan loosely and
reduce the heat to low. Cook for 4–6 minutes until the egg whites are
set but yolks still soft (or longer, to taste).

Alternatively, you can beat the eggs and stir them into the sauce for
the scrambled version, which is common in mountain homes.

Garnish with a few mint leaves or parsley if you like, then serve
immediately in the pan to share at the table. Beid w Banadoura is best
eaten hot, scooped up with fresh Lebanese khobez, pita or markouk
alongside olives, fresh mint, and radishes.

Notes...

For the best flavour, use ripe, local tomatoes –
or San Marzano or Kumato tomatoes if local
varieties are out of season.

If the tomatoes are very acidic, a pinch of
sugar balances the sauce.

In the Békaa – a valley in eastern Lebanon
– some families add a little chopped green
chilli or fresh za'atar leaves.

Balila
بليلة

Chickpeas, olive oil & lemon broth
Serves 4–5

500g dried chickpeas (or 2 x 400g jars of good quality chickpeas)

2 tsp bicarbonate of soda (for soaking and cooking)

4 garlic cloves, finely grated

Juice of 2 large lemons, or to taste

1½ tsp fine sea salt, or to taste

¼ tsp freshly ground black pepper

1 tsp ground cumin, plus extra to sprinkle on top

80ml extra virgin olive oil, plus extra for drizzling

1 tsp Aleppo pepper or paprika (optional)

2 tbsp finely chopped fresh parsley

Balila is one of those humble dishes that says everything about Lebanese breakfast: warm, honest, and nourishing. I remember my father sitting at the table in the early morning, tearing pieces of fresh pita, scooping warm chickpeas glistening with olive oil, and squeezing just a little more lemon – 'to wake it up', he used to say. It's a dish that speaks to our roots, to the mountain homes and old Beirut kitchens, where garlic, lemon, and cumin come together like old friends. Nothing fancy: just real food, made with care and meant to be shared.

Soak the dried chickpeas overnight in a large bowl of water with 1 teaspoon of the bicarbonate of soda. Drain and rinse thoroughly the next day. Transfer to a large pot, add the remaining teaspoon of bicarbonate and mix well. Cover with plenty of fresh water and bring to the boil. Skim off any foam and loose skins, then reduce the heat and simmer for 1.5–2 hours until the chickpeas are tender and buttery. Drain while still warm.

In a large bowl, combine the warm chickpeas with the grated garlic, lemon juice, sea salt, black pepper, and cumin. Add the extra virgin olive oil and toss gently to coat. Taste and adjust the seasoning with more lemon or salt if needed – it should be lemony and bold.

Transfer to a serving dish, drizzle with more olive oil, sprinkle with extra cumin or Aleppo pepper, and finish with a generous handful of finely chopped fresh parsley. Serve warm with fresh Lebanese khobez and crunchy vegetables such as radish, cucumber, and tomato or pickles on the side, the proper Lebanese way.

E'jjeh
عجة بالأعشاب

Lebanese herby egg fritters
Serves 4–5

40g flat-leaf parsley, finely chopped (1 large bunch)

20g fresh dill, finely chopped (about ½ bunch)

15g fresh mint leaves, finely chopped

80g spring onion, finely chopped

6 large free-range eggs

1½ tbsp plain flour (about 15g)

1 tsp baking powder

½ tsp bicarbonate of soda

2 garlic cloves, finely grated

1½ tsp fine sea salt, or to taste

¼ tsp freshly ground black pepper

1 tsp Baharat (Lebanese 7 spices)

Rapeseed oil, for shallow frying (approx. 250–300ml)

E'jjeh was never just breakfast, lunch, or dinner – it was a 'between' meal. A quick fix when the pantry was low, or when neighbours came over and something had to be made that was fast but generous. In our southern village, you'd smell it frying across balconies on Fridays after noon prayers. My mother would make it after the souk, when the herbs were freshest – parsley from our garden, dill and mint from the neighbours. We didn't eat it alone. She'd send a plate across the street to our Aunt Hwaida, and another to the old couple downstairs. We'd eat it hot with pickled radish and laban, sitting on the balcony floor, watching the breeze shake the fig trees.

Wash all the fresh herbs and spring onions thoroughly in cold water with a splash of vinegar or pinch of salt. Soak, rinse twice more, and then dry completely.

Crack the eggs into a large bowl and whisk until light and fluffy. Add the flour, baking powder and bicarbonate of soda, then whisk again until smooth. Mix in the garlic, salt, pepper, and Baharat before folding in the parsley, dill, mint, and spring onion. The batter should be thick and vibrant, heavy with herbs. Let it rest for 5–10 minutes to hydrate and deepen in flavour.

Heat 1cm of rapeseed oil in a wide frying pan over medium heat. Drop a spoonful of the mixture into the hot oil and shape into small rounds. Fry for 1–2 minutes per side until puffed, golden, and crisp on the edges. Don't crowd the pan. Remove with a slotted spoon and drain on kitchen paper.

Serve the e'jjeh hot or warm — either way, they'll disappear quickly! Plate them with labneh, olives, pickled wild cucumbers, and fresh markouk or khobez. They're also perfect tucked into warm bread with radish, tomato, and a dash of salt — the kind of sandwich you'd take with you on a picnic or to the fields.

Notes...

This mixture can be made up to 4 hours ahead and fried just before serving.

In the South, some families add shankleesh cheese crumbs to the batter for a stronger, tangier flavour.

Beid w Awarma
بيض و قاورما

Lebanese eggs with preserved lamb
confit & pomegranate molasses
Serves 4–5

For the awarma
(makes 2 small jars)

300g minced lamb fat (ideally tail fat
(liyyeh) or lamb belly fat)

800g shoulder or leg of good quality
grass-fed lamb, trimmed and cut into
1.5cm cubes

1½ tbsp fine sea salt, or to taste

1 tsp freshly ground black pepper

1 tsp Baharat (Lebanese 7 spices)

Small pinch of cinnamon (optional, used
in some families' recipes)

For the dish

150–200g Lebanese awarma (see above)

1 tsp samneh or ghee (optional, for extra
richness)

7–8 large free-range eggs

½ tsp fine sea salt

¼ tsp freshly ground black pepper

1 tsp Baharat (Lebanese 7 spices)

1 tbsp pomegranate molasses

Notes...

The quality of the awarma is everything; the
lamb must be slow-cooked and preserved
properly in its own fat. Homemade is best,
but Mymouné or artisan butchers are
excellent sources in the UK if you would
prefer to buy it.

Beid w Awarma is not just food; it's tradition, survival, and
love sealed in fat. My grandfather used to make the awarma
every autumn, lamb slowly cooked in its own fat and packed
into clay jars to last the winter. My mum would scoop a
spoonful into a pan on cold mornings, and we'd wait for
the scent to drift through the house. She'd crack in the eggs
and cook them gently, never rushing. Neighbours would
smell it and shout, 'Fee beid w awarma 'endkon?' and she'd
always send over a portion. It's a dish you eat slowly, with
warm bread, laughter, and strong tea.

To prepare the awarma

In a heavy pot, slowly render the fat over very low heat for about
30–40 minutes, until clear and golden. Strain out any solids. Return
the liquid fat to the pot.

Add the cubed lamb, salt, pepper, and spices. Keep the heat very low
– the meat should simmer slowly, never fry. Let it cook uncovered for
1.5–2 hours, stirring now and then. Moisture will evaporate, leaving
tender meat submerged in fat.

Once ready, spoon into sterilised jars. Ensure the meat is fully covered
with fat – this is key for preservation. Let it cool completely before
storing in the fridge, where it will keep for months.

To assemble and cook

Scoop the desired amount of awarma from the jar, including both
meat and fat. If it has been refrigerated, let it sit at room temperature
for 10 minutes to soften the fat slightly.

In a wide non-stick or traditional clay pan (sajiyyeh), heat the awarma
gently over medium-low heat until the fat melts and the lamb pieces
begin to sizzle and release their aroma, about 2–3 minutes. Add the
samneh if using.

Crack the eggs directly into the pan, spacing them out evenly. Reduce
the heat to low and cover the pan loosely with a lid or foil. Cook for
4–6 minutes, depending on how soft or firm you like the yolks. Avoid
stirring — this dish is best with whole eggs.

Sprinkle with the salt, black pepper, and Baharat. Remove from the
heat once the whites are set and yolks still soft, then drizzle with the
pomegranate molasses.

Serve directly in the pan, always with something to dip into the
golden fat. Beid w Awarma is meant to be shared from the pan,
eaten with hands and torn bread. Pair it with green olives, fresh mint,
radishes, and hot tea or laban. Traditionally served for breakfast or
early lunch, especially in cold mountain homes.

Mana'eesh Za'atar
مناقيش زعتر

Baked wild thyme, sumac & sesame
flatbread
Serves 4–5 | Makes 5 medium flatbreads

For the dough
See the recipe for Mana'eesh Banadoura
on page 41

For the za'atar mixture
5 tbsp Lebanese za'atar blend (thyme-
heavy, with sumac and sesame – see
below to make your own)

100ml extra virgin olive oil (the best
quality you can find)

Pinch of Aleppo pepper or chilli flakes for
extra heat (optional)

To make your own za'atar blend (approx. 250g)
120g dried wild za'atar (preferably za'atar
barri from a Lebanese grocer or your own
dried thyme)

50g white sesame seeds, lightly toasted
in a dry pan

60g ground sumac (it should be deep red
and tangy)

1 tsp dried marjoram (optional)

1 tsp fine sea salt, or to taste

There's a reason mana'eesh za'atar smells like Lebanon in the morning. Not just because it's everywhere in Beirut's side-street bakeries, or on a mountain breakfast table, but because of the story behind it, and how deeply rooted it is in our soil. This dough, topped with your own téh'wijé (blend) of wild thyme, sesame and sumac mixed to a paste with bold, green southern olive oil, isn't just breakfast. It's the land in your hands. It's your family. It's your Lebanon.

To prepare the za'atar mixture
In a small bowl, combine the za'atar with the olive oil. It should have a loose, spreadable texture, not too thick and not too runny. Add a pinch of Aleppo pepper or chilli if desired.

To assemble and bake
Preheat your oven to 220°C (200°C fan) with a heavy tray or pizza stone inside.

Divide the dough into 5 equal balls and roll each into a 20cm round. Lay on parchment paper. Brush each round with melted butter or olive oil if desired for extra richness. Spread 1.5–2 tablespoons of the za'atar mixture onto each, spreading it to the edges in a thin, even layer. Transfer to the hot oven and bake for 8–10 minutes, or until the edges are lightly golden and the za'atar is bubbling slightly.

To serve
Serve hot or warm, folded or open. Best enjoyed with labneh, fresh vegetables such as radishes, cucumber and tomatoes, and olives on the side. Eat with the hands, tearing and dipping, talking between bites.

Mana'eesh Kishek
مناقيش كشك

Baked fermented yoghurt & burghul
flatbread
Serves 4–5 | Makes 5 medium flatbreads

For the dough
See the recipe for Mana'eesh Banadoura
on page 41

For the kishek topping
5 tbsp kishek powder

1 medium brown onion, very finely
chopped

1 medium vine tomato, finely chopped

1 garlic clove, finely grated

4 tbsp extra virgin olive oil

2–3 tbsp lukewarm water

1 tsp fine sea salt, or to taste

½ tsp freshly ground black pepper

Finely chopped fresh red chilli (optional)

Kishek was never bought, it was made. That strong, sour, tangy smell would fill the kitchen at the end of summer when Mum and Teta would start the process. Mixing laban with fine burghul and salt, kneading it daily, spreading it on cloth-lined trays on the rooftop to dry under the southern sun. Each morning, it was turned over with care, the scent of fermentation rising slowly. We knew not to touch it. Only the women were allowed near. Later, once dried and brittle, it was ground into fine powder and poured into large glass jars, to be kept in the pantry, wrapped in cloth, far from the light. That kishek would feed us all winter. Stirred into soups, rolled into raw onion and olive oil, or best of all spread on dough and baked.

Mana'eesh kishek is underrated, forgotten by many, but in the mountain villages it's a sacred tradition. It's the memory of long summers, of mothers working with the seasons, and of survival wrapped in flavour. It's the kind of manou'sheh that doesn't shout, it whispers to those who understand. Despite its incredible nutritional profile and deep cultural value, kishek remains underappreciated in the UK for a few reasons. One is unfamiliarity, as many people don't know what it is or how to use it. Another is the misunderstood aroma; the sour, fermented smell can be off-putting to someone unfamiliar with Levantine food. And a lack of context: without understanding its story and tradition, kishek appears simple, even plain, so storytelling is essential.

To prepare the kishek topping
In a bowl, mix all the ingredients together. The consistency should be like thick paste – spreadable but not runny. Taste it. You want tanginess, umami, and a soft onion hit. Add fresh chilli to taste if desired.

To assemble and bake
Preheat your oven to 220°C (200°C fan) with a heavy tray or pizza stone inside.

Divide the dough into 5 equal balls. Roll each into a round about 20cm in diameter on a lightly floured surface, then place each round on parchment paper.

Spread 2–3 tablespoons of the kishek mixture on each round of dough, going right to the edges.

Bake for 10–12 minutes, or until the edges are golden and the topping lightly browned.

Serve hot with labneh, olives, mint leaves, or just as it is – folded, torn, or whole. A glass of hot black tea on the side completes the picture.

Mana'eesh Jibneh
مناقيش جبنة

Baked halloumi & Akkawi cheese
flatbread
Serves 4–5 | Makes 5 medium flatbreads

Mana'eesh is not just food. It's habit. It's memory. It's
identity. It's knowing that somewhere out there, someone
else is spreading cheese on dough just like you, waiting
for the heat of a baker's oven to turn it into something
comforting and familiar. That's what mana'eesh means to
me. Not just a recipe, but a ritual that belongs to all of us.

For the dough

See the recipe for Mana'eesh Banadoura
on page 41

For the topping

250g Akkawi cheese, soaked in cold
water for 2–3 hours

150g halloumi cheese, soaked in cold
water for 2–3 hours

1–2 tbsp olive oil (to bind the cheese mix)

3 tbsp melted unsalted butter or olive oil
(for brushing the dough)

Finely chopped fresh mint or wild
za'atar leaves and toasted sesame seeds
(optional)

To serve

Fresh tomatoes, quartered

Lebanese olives (green or black)

Mint leaves

Hot black tea with fresh mint

To prepare the cheese topping

Drain the Akkawi and halloumi cheeses well and pat dry. Crumble
them with your hands and mix together. Add enough olive oil to
gently bind the cheeses. You can mix in a bit of fresh mint or wild
thyme for added aroma if you like.

To assemble and bake

Preheat your oven to 220°C (200°C fan) with a heavy tray or pizza
stone inside.

Divide the dough into 5 equal balls. Roll each into a round about
20cm in diameter on a lightly floured surface.

Place each round on parchment paper. Before topping the dough,
brush the surface of each flattened round with the melted butter or
olive oil — this keeps the base tender and adds a golden finish.

Spread a generous amount of the cheese mixture over the top,
leaving a 1cm border all around. Sprinkle with toasted sesame seeds
if you like.

Transfer to the hot oven (ideally onto the stone or preheated tray) and
bake for 10–12 minutes, or until the dough is cooked through, golden
at the edges, and the cheese is bubbling and slightly browned.

To serve

Serve hot and folded, or open as is, with the tomatoes, olives, and
mint on the side. Perfect with black tea infused with fresh mint. Eat
with the hands, while warm, as it was meant to be.

Mana'eesh Banadoura

مناقيش بندورة

Baked tomato, onion, sumac & olive oil flatbread

Serves 4–5 | Makes 5 medium flatbreads

For the dough

1 tsp dried active yeast

1 tsp sugar

150ml lukewarm water

150ml lukewarm whole milk

500g strong white bread flour

1 tsp fine sea salt

2 tbsp olive oil, plus extra for kneading and resting

For the banadoura topping

500g vine-ripened red tomatoes, peeled and grated or finely chopped

1 medium red onion, very finely chopped

1 tbsp tomato paste (optional, for depth)

2 tbsp extra virgin olive oil

1½ tsp fine sea salt, or to taste

1 tsp Aleppo pepper or chilli flakes, or to taste

1 tsp smoked paprika

1 tsp dried mint

1 tsp sumac

1 tsp pomegranate molasses

Mana'eesh Banadoura is the unsung hero of the Lebanese breakfast. Humble, bold, packed with sunshine and spice. In our village, it was the summer version of mana'eesh, when tomatoes were bursting with juice and every home had bowls ready for breakfast or lunch. It's a recipe full of improvisation, yet deeply traditional – made by farmers, fishermen, housewives, always with what the land offered.

To prepare the dough

In a small bowl, mix the yeast, sugar, water, and milk together. Let it sit for 10 minutes until it becomes frothy and active.

In a large mixing bowl or stand mixer, combine the flour and salt. Gradually pour in the yeast mixture and olive oil. Knead by hand or with a dough hook for about 8–10 minutes until soft, smooth, and elastic.

Cover the bowl with a clean cloth and leave to rise for 1–1.5 hours in a warm place, or until doubled in size.

To prepare the topping

In a bowl, combine all the ingredients. The mixture should be loose but not watery. The grated tomatoes will soften the onion as they sit. Taste and adjust the salt or heat.

To assemble and bake

Preheat your oven to 220°C (200°C fan) with a heavy tray or pizza stone inside.

Divide the dough into 5 equal balls. Roll each into a round about 20cm in diameter on a lightly floured surface, then place each round on parchment paper.

Spread 2–3 tablespoons of the tomato mixture evenly on each round of dough, going close to the edges.

Transfer the mana'eesh to the hot oven using baking parchment or a pizza peel. Bake for 10–12 minutes, until the edges are golden and the topping is bubbling and slightly caramelised at the edges.

Serve hot or warm, folded or open. Add a few fresh mint leaves or serve with olives and cucumber slices. Some wrap it around halloumi or a fried egg. It's perfect as is though – honest, fragrant, alive with Lebanese summer.

Lahém b'Ajine
لحم بعجين

Golden baked flatbread with spiced minced lamb
Serves 4–5 | Makes 5 medium flatbreads

For the dough
See the recipe for Mana'eesh Banadoura on page 41

For the meat topping
400g minced lamb (ask your butcher for lean, twice-minced shoulder or leg) or a mix of lamb and beef

2 medium tomatoes, grated or blended

1 medium brown onion, finely grated or blended

3 garlic cloves, finely grated

1½ tbsp tomato paste

1½ tbsp pomegranate molasses

1 tsp smoked paprika

1 tsp Baharat (Lebanese 7 spices)

½ tsp Aleppo pepper or chilli flakes

½ tsp freshly ground black pepper

1 tbsp fine sea salt, or to taste

This dish doesn't just remind me of the kitchen, it reminds me of the road, the smell of pine trees, the hum of the car engine heading south. We would buy dozens of small lahém b'ajine on summer or weekend trips, each the size of a hand, bubbling hot, edges crisp, the meat fragrant with tomato and pomegranate molasses. In every Lebanese town, whether in Saida, Nabatieh, or the Békaa, you'll find a version of this dish. Some make it fiery, others milder. But the soul remains the same: dough, meat, spice, and a memory tucked into each bite.

To prepare the topping
Combine all the ingredients in a bowl. Mix thoroughly by hand – the mixture should be loose but not runny. If it feels dry, add a spoonful of tomato juice or a bit more molasses. Leave to rest for 10–15 minutes to let the flavours come together.

To assemble and bake
Preheat your oven to 220°C (200°C fan) with a heavy tray or pizza stone inside.

Divide the dough into 5 equal balls. Roll each into a round about 20cm in diameter on a lightly floured surface, then place each round on parchment paper.

Spread about 3 tablespoons of the meat mixture evenly over each round of dough, going right to the edges. The topping should be thin but fully cover the surface.

Bake for 10–12 minutes on the tray or pizza stone, until the meat is cooked and the edges are golden.

Serve hot with lemon wedges, fresh mint, pickled turnips, and a small bowl of laban. Some fold it, others eat it open. It's perfect wrapped and eaten on the go or shared at a long table with chatter and tea.

Mezza at Home

Mezza that stayed at home – what we really eat

Not all mezza made it to the restaurants. Some never even made it past the front door. These are the quiet dishes, the ones that never got dressed up for the spotlight, but in every Lebanese home, they are the heartbeat of the table.

This chapter is for the food we grew up with. The dishes that never needed a menu or a guest to justify them, that were made simply because we were hungry and Mum had thirty minutes to feed a house full of people. Think of it as the intimate side of the mezza story – one you'll rarely find in cookbooks, and almost never on restaurant tables.

Here you'll find kibbét batata, a humble, earthy mix of mashed potato and burghul seasoned with olive oil and sweet onion, eaten cold, scooped up with warm bread, and always with raw spring onion on the side. And kibbét banadoura, too, a tomato and burghul tartare that's juicy, spicy, and fresh – our summer comfort food.

There's ful akhdar, young green fava beans sautéed with garlic and coriander, eaten warm or cold with a squeeze of lemon and salt – the kind of dish that appears at lunch without anyone asking and disappears even faster. Batata w beid – fried potatoes with eggs cracked over them straight in the pan, the edges crisping up in olive oil – is another staple that's fast, cheap, and unbeatable. And, of course, sawda djej: bold, rich, sweet-sour chicken liver fried with pomegranate molasses. Not a dish you eat on a date, but always fought over with your siblings!

These dishes are rarely photographed. They don't have a set presentation, and you'll never find them garnished with micro herbs. But they're the food that built us. This is what was on our tables on a random Tuesday, not just for Eid or a Sunday feast. It's what we made after school, what was packed in foil for the beach, what was cooked quickly between power cuts.

So here they are – finally written down, shared the way we make them. Designed to satisfy, not to impress. No flourishes. Just the food we really eat, the way we really eat it.

Shorbet Djej
with Vermicelli
شوربة دجاج

Soothing Lebanese chicken & vermicelli
soup
Serves 4–6

Traditional, comforting, and cooked the way my family's
been doing it for generations – shorbet djej is the taste of
home when you're unwell, the warmth of being looked after.
I still remember the scent drifting from the kitchen when I
came home tired or cold: a whole chicken gently simmering
with cinnamon, onions, and a touch of love. My mother
always said it 'warms the heart before the body'. We ate it
boiling hot, squeezing lemon juice and cracking fresh black
pepper on top. It wasn't just soup – it was healing.

For the broth

1–1.2kg whole chicken

3–3.5L cold water

1 large onion, peeled and halved

1 celery stalk (optional, for depth of
flavour)

4 whole black peppercorns

2–4 bay leaves

1 cinnamon stick

2 cloves

1 tbsp fine sea salt, or to taste

For the soup

4 tbsp olive oil or samneh

120g wheat vermicelli noodles, broken
into 2–3cm pieces

1 medium brown onion, finely chopped

2 garlic cloves, finely grated

½ tsp ground cinnamon

1 tsp Baharat (Lebanese 7 spices)

Fine sea salt and freshly ground black
pepper, to taste

Juice of 1 large lemon

Start by preparing the chicken. If using a whole bird, rinse it under
cold water and remove any visible offal, liver, or heart from the cavity.
Trim away excess fat and check for pinfeathers. Some families also
like to rub the chicken briefly with lemon juice and a pinch of salt,
then rinse again — this helps to remove any lingering odour and is a
common traditional step in Lebanese kitchens.

Place the cleaned chicken in a large pot and cover it with the cold
water. Bring to a boil over medium heat. As it starts boiling, you'll
notice greyish foam rising to the surface — use a spoon to skim this
off, keeping the broth clear and clean. Once the water is simmering
gently, add the halved onion, celery (if using), peppercorns, bay
leaves, cinnamon stick, cloves, and salt. Lower the heat, cover
partially, and let it simmer gently for 50–60 minutes, or until the
chicken is fully cooked and tender.

Once done, remove the chicken and set it aside to cool slightly. Strain
the broth through a fine sieve into a clean pot or bowl, discarding the
solids. When the chicken is cool enough, remove the skin and bones,
and shred the meat into bite-size pieces.

In a large soup pot, heat the olive oil or samneh over medium heat.
Add the vermicelli and toast it, stirring constantly, until golden brown
– this only takes a few minutes, so don't step away. Once golden,
add the chopped onion and sauté for 4–5 minutes until soft. Add the
garlic and cook for another 30 seconds until fragrant. Sprinkle in the
ground cinnamon, Baharat, and a pinch of salt and pepper.

Now pour in about 2 litres of your prepared chicken broth and bring
it to a gentle simmer. Add the shredded chicken and cook everything
together for about 15–20 minutes, until the vermicelli is soft but still
holds its shape. Taste and adjust the seasoning – you might need a
touch more salt, depending on how much the broth reduced during
simmering.

Right before serving, stir in the lemon juice. The lemon lifts the soup
beautifully and gives it that bright, homey touch that every Lebanese
Teta would approve of.

Serve it hot, with Lebanese khobez on the side.

Adass bil Hamod
عدس بالحامض

Lemony green lentil & Swiss chard soup
Serves 4–5

250g green lentils

1.5–1.8L water, or vegetable stock if you have it

4–5 tbsp extra virgin olive oil

1 medium brown onion, finely chopped

5–6 garlic cloves, finely grated

1 medium potato, peeled and diced into small cubes

1 tbsp fine sea salt, or to taste

½ tbsp freshly ground black pepper

300g Swiss chard, washed and drained

Juice of 2–3 lemons (approx. 60–80ml)

Adass bil hamod was always the smell of home on a rainy afternoon – the pot simmering quietly while Mum added the lemon, the silver spoon tasting every few minutes. A mountain dish and true comfort food for us. We ate it with torn bread, a drizzle of olive oil, and always around the table, never rushed. Simple, humble, but it hugs you from the inside out. This is the real home-style version with all the details and love, just how I would make it at home.

Start by rinsing your green lentils properly: give them a good wash in cold water to remove any dust and debris, repeating 2 or 3 times until the water runs clear. Add the rinsed lentils to a large pot with 1.5 litres of water or stock. Bring it to the boil and then reduce the heat to a simmer. Skim off the foam and let the lentils cook for about 30 minutes, or until they are mostly tender but not mushy.

While the lentils are cooking, heat the olive oil in a frying pan over medium heat. Sauté the onion until it softens and becomes golden, add the garlic and cook for another 3–4 minutes until softened. Add this mixture to the pot with the lentils.

Add the potatoes to the pot along with the salt and black pepper. Let everything simmer together for about 20–25 minutes until the potatoes are soft and the lentils are fully cooked through. If the soup thickens too much, you can always add a little more water or stock to maintain the texture.

Now, take the Swiss chard and separate the stems from the leaves. Chop the stems into small pieces first, as they take longer to cook. Add them to the soup, let them soften for about 5 minutes, then throw in the roughly chopped leaves. Let them wilt and cook for another 5–10 minutes.

Finish the soup with the lemon juice, adjusting to taste. Some people love it tangy, others less so. Add more salt if needed and then stir well.

Serve hot, with a side of Lebanese khobez and a few olives for extra flavour.

Sawda Ghanam
سودة غنم مقلية

Lamb livers seared with garlic, lemon &
Baharat
Serves 4–5

500g lamb liver (ask your butcher for
very fresh, firm liver with the membrane
removed)

4 tbsp extra virgin olive oil

5 garlic cloves, finely grated

1½ tsp fine sea salt, or to taste

½ tsp freshly ground black pepper, or to
taste

½ tsp Baharat (Lebanese 7 spices)

¼ tsp chilli flakes or 1 small fresh red chilli
(optional)

Juice of 1 lemon

Fresh chopped parsley, to garnish

This dish takes me back to those early mornings when my
father would come home from the butcher with fresh sawda
wrapped in butcher's paper, still warm. My mother always
said it had to be cooked the same day, no refrigeration, just
cleaned well and straight into the pan. She'd rinse it with
lemon juice, pat it dry, and sauté it with garlic, lemon juice,
a little Baharat, and a kiss of heat. We'd eat it with fresh
bread, fresh mint, and raw spring onion on the side. It's the
food of real people – honest, warm, and full of soul. Just
like many things in our culture, it's meant to be shared.

Clean the liver well and trim off any connective tissue or small veins.
Slice into bite-size strips, about 1cm thick. Pat dry thoroughly with
kitchen paper to help it sear properly rather than steaming.

Heat the olive oil in a wide sauté pan over medium-high heat. Once
hot, add the liver pieces in a single layer (do not overcrowd the pan).
Let them sear undisturbed for about 2–3 minutes to develop colour,
then flip and cook the other side for another 2–3 minutes. The liver
should be browned on the outside but still tender and just slightly
pink inside – if overcooked it will become dry and tough.

Add the garlic, salt, black pepper, Baharat, and chilli (if using) to the
pan. Sauté for another 30 seconds until the garlic is fragrant. Finally,
squeeze over the lemon juice and stir briefly to coat the liver.

Transfer immediately to a serving plate, drizzle with a touch more
olive oil, and garnish with fresh parsley.

Serve with warm Lebanese khobez, classic sides – raw onions,
radishes, fresh mint – and, if it's evening, a small glass of arak.

Fraké Nayyé
فرَكي نيّة

Southern-style spiced lamb tartare
Serves 4–5

600g very lean fresh lamb leg or
shoulder meat, butchered the same day

1 small brown onion, very finely grated

2 fresh red chillies, deseeded and finely
chopped

2 tbsp téh'wijé spice blend (see page 54)

1 tsp fine sea salt, or to taste

½ tsp freshly ground black pepper

4–5 tbsp extra virgin olive oil

Ice cubes, for kneading and keeping meat
cool

To serve

2 tbsp extra virgin olive oil

Warm Lebanese khobez

3–4 whole spring onions

4–5 fresh mint sprigs

4–5 whole radishes

This dish is a true specialty of the South. Fraké nayyé isn't
just food, it's an occasion. Families gather around the table,
the lamb is freshly butchered and carefully minced by hand.
It is kneaded slowly with téh'wijé spices, onion, chilli, and
olive oil until it becomes silky, almost creamy in texture.
Eaten with fresh warm bread, spring onions, mint, and a
glass of arak, it's one of those bold Lebanese traditions that
carries stories of villages, resilience, and togetherness.

Start by making sure the lamb is fresh, lean, and has been very finely
minced using a powerful food processor or the butcher's mincer on
the day you plan to serve this dish. Place the meat in a large, chilled
bowl. Add the grated onion, finely chopped chillies, téh'wijé spice
blend, salt, and pepper.

Using your hands (which should be washed and cold), begin kneading
the meat gently, dipping your fingers in iced water as you work to
keep the mixture cool and smooth. Slowly add the olive oil as you
knead, letting it emulsify into the lamb. Continue until the mixture
feels silky and cohesive.

Once ready, divide the mixture into equal portions (about the size of
a small orange). Take one portion at a time and press it firmly into the
palm of your hand, shaping it into a roughly oval patty. The pressure
of your fingers will naturally leave shallow grooves across the surface
– this is the traditional southern signature. Repeat with all portions.

Arrange them on a wide platter and drizzle lightly with more olive oil.
Serve immediately with fresh khobez, spring onions, mint leaves, and
radishes. A glass of arak is the traditional companion.

Notes...

Freshness is everything – fraké nayyé must be
made and eaten the same day.

Always knead by hand with iced water nearby
to prevent the meat from heating and to
achieve the silky texture.

The téh'wijé adds depth and identity – don't
skip it.

Kibbet Banadoura
كبة بندورة

*Juicy tomato kibbé from the
south of Lebanon*
Serves 4–5

For the base

250g fine brown burghul

3–4 large ripe heritage vine tomatoes
(they should be very soft and juicy)

1 small brown onion, grated

1 tbsp tomato paste

1½ tsp fine sea salt, or to taste

½ tsp freshly ground black pepper

½ tsp ground cumin

60–80ml extra virgin olive oil

For the téh'wijé

10–15 fresh mint leaves

10–15 fresh basil leaves

5g fresh marjoram

1 fresh red chilli (use a mild or hot variety
to taste and deseed if preferred)

1–2g edible dried rose petals, gently
crushed (optional, for fragrance and
depth)

Now we're talking real southern roots. No true Kibbet Banadoura from Jabal Amel comes to life without the soul of the dish, the téh'wijé – that special, fragrant herb mix that gives the raw kibbé its unique flavour, identity, and memory. In the southern hills of Lebanon, this dish isn't written in books, it's passed down by taste, by scent, by watching Teta crush herbs with her hands.

Kibbet Banadoura is the humblest yet most soulful kibbeh of our land – the flavour of barefoot summers, clay bowls, and mountain silence. No meat. No fire. No frills or tricks. Just the purest fruits of the earth: sun-warmed tomatoes, hand-picked herbs, and olive oil pressed from your neighbour's trees. It's eaten fresh with romaine leaves or warm bread, and usually in good company, around a table full of stories.

To prepare the base

Rinse the burghul well under cold water. Soak for 10–15 minutes until it softens, then squeeze it dry with your hands or using a muslin cloth. It should be fluffy, not wet.

Grate the ripe tomatoes into a wide mixing bowl using a box grater, keeping all the juice and discarding the skins. Add the grated onion and tomato paste, then season with salt, pepper, and cumin. Mix gently.

To prepare the téh'wijé

Ensure all your herbs are fresh, washed well, and dried thoroughly. Finely chop the mint, basil, marjoram, and chilli. Combine them into one fragrant, colourful blend along with the rose petals, if using.

Add the téh'wijé directly into the tomato bowl. Stir gently to blend.

To finish the kibbé

Add the soaked, drained burghul to the tomato and herb mixture. Begin kneading with clean hands for about 5–7 minutes, just as our mothers did. The mix should become cohesive, smooth, and slightly sticky, not watery or dry. Adjust the salt and spice to taste. Let it rest for 5 minutes.

Just before serving, drizzle with extra virgin olive oil and gently mix. Plate in a shallow dish, flatten the surface with the back of a spoon, and decorate with a few mint or basil leaves if you like. Serve immediately with crisp romaine leaves or warm khobez, and a few raw onion wedges for those who know how to eat it right.

Kibbet Batata
كبة بطاطا

Mashed potato kibbé with burghul, herbs
& onions
Serves 4–5

For the kibbé base

500g potatoes (a floury, starchy variety
like Maris Piper or King Edward)

150g fine brown burghul

1 small brown onion, finely grated

1½ tsp fine sea salt, or to taste

1 tsp ground cumin

½ tsp freshly ground black pepper

¼ tsp Aleppo pepper, for mild heat

60–80ml extra virgin olive oil

4–5 tbsp water, as needed

For the téh'wijé

See the recipe for Kibbet Banadoura
on page 54

A humble, warm, and comforting dish that truly belongs
to every Lebanese home. But for us, this isn't just kibbé
made with potatoes. This is a poor man's feast, a vegetarian
heirloom born from love, ingenuity, and simplicity. It's
often made in the South and parts of the Békaa, especially
during Lent, or simply when there's no meat on the table,
and no one complains. Because when seasoned right, folded
with olive oil and herbs, and paired with good olives and
pickles, it's soul food.

Boil the potatoes whole in salted water until fully soft, about 20–25
minutes. Drain, peel and mash them while still warm, until smooth
without any lumps. Leave to cool slightly.

While the potatoes boil, soak the fine burghul in just enough water to
cover it for 10 minutes. Drain and squeeze dry using your hands or a
muslin cloth. Set aside.

In a large bowl, combine the mashed potato, burghul, onion, salt,
and spices. Mix well by hand, then add the téh'wijé and stir gently
to blend. Continue mixing or kneading gently for 3–5 minutes while
adding the olive oil and water slowly until you have a soft, cohesive
dough that's fragrant and pliable.

Taste and adjust the seasoning with more salt if needed. Press into a
shallow serving dish, using wet hands to smooth the surface. Drizzle
generously with olive oil and serve at room temperature with pickles,
olives, and warm Lebanese khobez.

This kibbé is the people's food, eaten with the hands, shared straight
from the plate. It can be kept at room temperature once made and
the older it gets, the deeper it tastes.

Shorbet Mawzet
.شوربة موزات

Lebanon's winter soup: lamb shank, rice
& rich broth
Serves 4–5

For the lamb and broth

1–1.2kg lamb shanks (about 4–5 pieces)

5–6L water

1 large brown onion, peeled and halved

3–4 bay leaves

1 cinnamon stick

6 black peppercorns

3 cloves

1 tbsp fine sea salt, or to taste

For the soup

2 tbsp samneh or olive oil

1 medium brown onion, finely chopped

2 garlic cloves, finely grated

1 medium carrot, diced

1 celery stalk, diced (optional)

1½ tsp Baharat (Lebanese 7 spices)

½ tsp freshly ground black pepper

½ tsp ground cinnamon

4 tbsp tomato paste

100g short grain rice

1½ tsp fine sea salt, or to taste

Juice of 1 large lemon

50g fresh parsley, chopped

This dish reminds me of quiet Sundays in the mountains. My father would bring fresh lamb shanks from the butcher in the souk early in the morning, and my mother would start simmering them with onions, cinnamon, and Baharat. The scent would fill the kitchen all day and meant something good was coming. By the time we sat to eat, the meat would fall off the bone, the broth would be rich and full of soul, and it was always served with fresh Lebanese bread. This isn't just soup; it's depth, comfort, and patience in a pot. Lebanese comfort food at its finest – slow, soulful, and full of meaning.

Begin by thoroughly cleaning the lamb shanks. Rinse them under cold water and pat them dry. You can soak them briefly in cold water with a splash of vinegar or lemon juice for 10 minutes, then rinse again to remove any gaminess and ensure a cleaner broth.

Place the lamb shanks in a large pot and cover them with the water. Slowly bring to a boil over medium heat, skimming off any scum that rises to the surface. Once the broth is clear, add the halved onion, bay leaves, cinnamon stick, peppercorns, cloves, and salt.

Lower the heat to a gentle simmer, partially cover the pot, and cook for 2–2.5 hours, or until the lamb is fall-off-the-bone tender. Remove the lamb shanks and set them aside. Strain the broth through a fine sieve and set aside separately.

In another large soup pot, heat the samneh or olive oil. Sauté the chopped onion until soft and lightly golden, then add the garlic, carrot, and celery (if using). Cook for a few more minutes until aromatic. Stir in the Baharat, black pepper, ground cinnamon, and tomato paste, then cook for another 2–4 minutes to bring out their richness.

Pour the strained lamb broth back into the pot and bring to a gentle simmer. Add the rice and simmer gently for about 18–20 minutes, until the grains are cooked through.

While the soup simmers, carefully remove the meat from the lamb shanks – leave some on the bone for presentation if you wish or shred it all into bite-size pieces. Add the lamb to the soup and simmer for another 5–10 minutes to bring all the flavours together. Taste and adjust the seasoning with salt and pepper.

Just before serving, stir in the lemon juice to brighten the broth and garnish with fresh parsley. You'll be left with a rich, thick soup where the lamb is meltingly tender, the rice has absorbed all the spiced broth, and each spoonful feels like a warm hug. Serve hot with warm Lebanese khobez, pickles (khiar and léfét), and lemon wedges for squeezing over each bowlful on the side.

Loubieh b Zeit
لوبية بزيت

Flat green beans simmered in tomatoes,
garlic & olive oil
Serves 4–5

600g Lebanese flat green beans (or fine
French beans)

5–6 large ripe tomatoes

100ml extra virgin olive oil

1 large brown onion, finely chopped

6–7 large garlic cloves, finely grated

1 tbsp tomato paste

1½ tbsp fine sea salt, or to taste

½ tsp freshly ground black pepper

1 tsp Baharat (Lebanese 7 spices)

One of the true pillars of Lebanese home cooking, Loubieh
b Zeit was a summer staple in my childhood, especially on
Fridays when the family gathered around the table for a
meatless lunch. Mum would sit on the veranda trimming
piles of green beans, chatting with neighbours passing by,
her hands moving faster than anyone else's. I remember
how she'd cook them slowly, lovingly, in the best olive oil,
with tomatoes just picked from the garden. It was always
served at room temperature, mopped up with bread, olives,
sweet onions and fresh green pepper on the side – sun, soil,
and oil on a plate.

Wash and trim the green beans, snapping them by hand to remove the
stringy ends. Peel the tomatoes by scoring the bottoms and blanching
briefly in boiling water to loosen the skins, then chop them finely.

In a wide, heavy pot, heat the olive oil over medium heat and sauté
the chopped onion until soft and translucent. Add the garlic and stir
until fragrant. Add the beans, toss well to coat them in the oil, then
stir in the chopped tomatoes and tomato paste. Season with salt,
black pepper, and Baharat.

Lower the heat and partially cover the pot. Let the beans simmer
gently in the tomato sauce for 40–50 minutes, stirring occasionally,
until they are meltingly tender and the oil has separated slightly from
the tomatoes. Taste and adjust the seasoning.

Let the dish cool to room temperature before serving, always
alongside warm Lebanese khobez, spring onions, and green pepper.

Notes...

Loubieh b Zeit is never rushed – the slower it
cooks, the better the flavour.

In the South, some families add a few whole
garlic cloves with the grated garlic.

Best eaten the same day it's made, at room
temperature, but leftovers are delicious cold
the next day with bread.

Ma'aalé
مقالي

Lebanon's favourite fried vegetables with
tarator & pomegranate
Serves 4–5

Ma'aalé was a Friday staple, a celebration of vegetables made with a simple but effective technique. I remember my mother frying each vegetable in its own time, carefully dusting the aubergine with flour so it wouldn't drink too much oil, layering them like a tapestry. Then came the garlic, the lemon, the creamy tahini, and the scattered pomegranate seeds that made the dish sing. A little mint and tomato salad on the side balanced it all. This is a dish built from patience, honouring each vegetable like a guest at the table.

For the vegetables

1 medium cauliflower, cut into small florets (about 600g)

2 medium courgettes, sliced lengthways into thick strips (350–400g)

1 medium aubergine, sliced into 1.5cm thick rounds (300–400g)

1–1.2L rapeseed oil, for shallow frying

2–3 tbsp plain flour, for dusting

1 tbsp fine sea salt, or to taste

1½ tsp freshly ground black pepper

1 tsp ground cumin

Seeds of ½ fresh pomegranate

2 tbsp chopped flat-leaf parsley, for garnish

For the tarator

See the recipe on page 202

For the salatet banadoura (tomato and cucumber salad)

3 ripe medium vine tomatoes, chopped into bite-size chunks

2 small Lebanese cucumbers, chopped into bite-size chunks

Large handful of fresh mint, leaves picked and roughly torn

Juice of 1 large lemon

2–3 tbsp extra virgin olive oil

1 tsp fine sea salt, or to taste

1 tsp sumac

To prepare the vegetables and tarator

Wash all the prepared vegetables thoroughly in cold water. Pat dry very well. Lightly salt the aubergine slices, season with black pepper and cumin, then set aside for 20 minutes. Meanwhile, make the tarator according to the recipe on page 202.

Preheat about 2–2.5cm oil in a wide frying pan over medium heat. Season the cauliflower florets and courgette strips, then fry in batches for 3–4 minutes per side until golden and just tender. Drain well on paper towels.

Pat the salted aubergine dry, then dust both sides with flour and shake off the excess. Fry for 3–4 minutes per side until deep golden. Drain on paper towels.

To prepare the salatet banadoura

Mix everything gently in a bowl just before serving to keep the tomatoes juicy but not soggy.

To serve

Arrange the fried vegetables layered or side-by-side on a platter. Spoon the tarator sauce generously over the top, then scatter with pomegranate seeds and chopped parsley. Serve the vegetables warm or at room temperature alongside the fresh tomato salad and warm Lebanese khobez.

Mjaddara Hamra
مجدّرة حمرا

Brown lentils & burghul with smoky
onions: the pride of the South
Serves 4–5

For the mjaddara hamra

250g brown lentils

1.2–1.4L water

150ml olive oil

4–5 medium brown onions, finely diced

1½ tsp ground cumin

1½ tsp fine sea salt, or to taste

½ tsp freshly ground black pepper

100g coarse brown burghul, washed
and drained

For the laban b'khyar

500g plain full-fat yoghurt (laban)

2 Lebanese cucumbers, finely diced

1 garlic clove, finely grated

½ tbsp dried mint

Fine sea salt, to taste

Notes...

The onions must be very dark but not burnt,
as this base gives the dish its signature colour
and flavour.

Cumin is always used to give the lentils and
burghul a bold flavour.

Laban b'khyar is an essential accompaniment
to balance the richness.

This dish is always served with bread –
families in Jezzine, Saida, and Marjeyoun
still eat it this way today.

In South Lebanon, mjaddara hamra is a dish that lives
in memory. In our old house, when the onions started to
fry, you could smell them all the way to the neighbours'
windows. My aunt Zahra always made this dish perfectly
– the grains fluffy, the onions dark and sweet, and a big
bowl of cold laban b'khyar on the side. This is not a dish of
shortcuts; it is simple but must be done with care and speak
of home.

To prepare the mjaddara hamra

Wash the lentils and place them in a large pot with about 1.2 litres
of the water. Bring to a boil, lower the heat, and simmer for 15–18
minutes, until just tender but still holding their shape – do not let
them overcook. Drain and reserve the cooking water.

Meanwhile, in a large pan, heat 120ml of the olive oil. Add the onions
and fry slowly over medium-low heat, stirring often, until very deeply
caramelised and dark golden brown (about 30–40 minutes).

When the onions are ready, carefully add the remaining water to the
pan. Stir well, scraping the bottom, and let it bubble gently for 2–3
minutes. This deglazing step lifts all the flavour from the pan and
creates a dark base.

Now add the drained lentils to the onions and stir gently to coat the
lentils with the onion base. Add about 400–500ml of the reserved
lentil cooking water. Season with the cumin, salt, and black pepper.
Bring to a boil.

Stir in the washed burghul. Mix well, cover tightly, lower the heat, and
cook very gently for 12–15 minutes until the burghul is tender, the
water has been absorbed, and the grains are fluffy, not wet or creamy.

Turn off the heat and let the mixture rest, covered, for 10 minutes.
Fluff gently with a fork so the lentils and burghul are separate, not
stuck together.

To prepare the laban b'khyar

In a bowl, whisk the yoghurt until smooth. Add the diced cucumbers,
grated garlic, dried mint, and salt to taste. Mix well and chill.

To serve

Spoon the mjaddara hamra onto a large platter. Fluff again gently.
Serve warm or at room temperature, with the laban b'khyar and
radishes, fresh mint, tomatoes, and plenty of khobez on the table.

Batata w Beid
بطاطا وبيض

Pan-fried potatoes & eggs with olive oil
& Baharat

Serves 4–5

700g Maris Piper or chipping potatoes

7 large free-range eggs

7 tbsp olive oil

4 garlic cloves, finely grated

1½ tsp fine sea salt, or to taste

1 tsp Baharat (Lebanese 7 spices)

½ tsp smoked paprika

2 spring onions, thinly sliced, green
parts only

Pinch of sumac (optional)

This dish was our emergency dinner and lazy Sunday brunch – always made in one pan, always satisfying. My mum would throw it together when she was tired or when we had guests drop in unexpectedly. It filled the kitchen with the smell of frying potatoes and garlic, and we'd tear fresh bread with our hands to scoop it up. This is true Lebanese comfort – humble, generous, and made with whatever we had.

Begin by washing and peeling the potatoes. Cut them into 1.5–2cm cubes and rinse in cold water to remove excess starch. Soak for 5–10 minutes, then drain and pat dry thoroughly with a clean towel. This helps them crisp up and cook evenly.

Place your eggs in a bowl, ready to crack into the pan later.

Heat the olive oil in a large non-stick pan over medium heat. Add the potatoes and sauté for 10–12 minutes, stirring occasionally, until golden and tender on the inside.

Add the garlic, salt, Baharat, and paprika. Stir well and cook for 1–2 more minutes until fragrant. The potatoes should be fully cooked and well-coated in spices.

Lower the heat slightly. Make 7 small wells in the potato mixture and carefully crack the eggs into them. Cover the pan with a lid and cook for 4–6 minutes, until the egg whites are set but the yolks are still soft, or longer if you prefer firm yolks. You can also beat the eggs lightly and pour them over the whole pan if you prefer a scrambled texture – both styles are traditional.

Remove from the heat and let it rest, uncovered, for a minute. Garnish with the spring onion and a sprinkle of sumac if you like.

Serve hot, straight from the pan, with warm Lebanese khobez. This goes perfectly with olives, pickles, and sliced cucumber or tomato.

Ful Maa'la Akhdar
فول أخضر

Green fava beans with garlic, coriander & lemon: the taste of early spring
Serves 4–5

600g fresh young green fava beans in the pod

80–100ml extra virgin olive oil

2 medium brown onions, thinly sliced

8–10 large garlic cloves, finely grated

1 small bunch fresh coriander, finely chopped (about 50g)

1½ tsp fine sea salt, or to taste

½ tsp freshly ground black pepper

Juice of 2 large lemons, or to taste

To serve
Lemon wedges

Lebanese khobez

Ful season was a short celebration, a few precious weeks when green fava beans were still soft and sweet. Mum never shelled them – instead, she'd sit outside in the sun, a big bowl in her lap, trimming the ends and snapping them into pieces with her hands. When they hit the pan with garlic, fresh coriander and olive oil, the whole house would fill with that unmistakable scent of spring. Ful maa'la wasn't just a side dish, it was the sign that winter was finally over.

Wash the fava bean pods thoroughly in cold water. Trim off the tough stem and tip of each pod and remove any stringy edges if needed. Cut each pod into 3–4cm pieces.

Heat the olive oil in a wide sauté pan. Add the sliced onion and cook until soft and golden, then add the garlic and cook until fragrant. Stir in the chopped coriander for 30 seconds. Add the fava beans, salt, and pepper.

Sauté over medium heat for 15–20 minutes, stirring occasionally, until the beans are tender and the pods are soft but not falling apart.

To finish the dish, add the lemon juice, stir well and adjust the seasoning to taste. Serve warm or at room temperature with lemon wedges and warm khobez.

Notes...
Only use young, tender fava bean pods – if the beans inside are large and the pods are fibrous, this cooking method won't work. You can find fresh green fava beans at Middle Eastern grocers and farmers' markets around the UK in spring.

This dish is best eaten the same day it's made, served slightly warm or at room temperature.

Salatet Halloum w Battikh

سلطة الحلوم والبطيخ

Grilled halloumi salad with watermelon, mint & olive oil

Serves 4–5

250g Lebanese-style halloumi cheese

500g ripe seedless watermelon, chilled

Small handful of fresh mint leaves (about 10g)

2 tbsp extra virgin olive oil

1 tbsp pomegranate molasses

1 tbsp freshly squeezed lemon juice

1 tbsp toasted sesame seeds

Pinch of Aleppo chilli flakes (optional, for a touch of heat)

This salad was our cold lunch during long, lazy summers in Beirut. We'd come home sunburnt from the sea, and my mum would slice the watermelon and fry halloum on the tiny gas burner she used to make coffee. The plate was always dripping with juice and olive oil, and we'd eat it with our hands, barefoot on the balcony under the grapevine.

Start by rinsing the halloum cheese under cold water to remove excess brine. Pat dry thoroughly with paper towels. Slice into slabs or strips, about 1cm thick – not too thin, or they'll melt while grilling.

Cut the watermelon into bite-size cubes or wedges. If it's not seedless, remove the seeds carefully with a small knife or spoon. Keep it chilled until the last minute so it stays firm.

Wash the mint leaves gently in cold water with a few drops of vinegar or lemon juice to refresh them and remove dust. Rinse and pat dry carefully. Tear the leaves by hand.

Heat a dry grill pan or non-stick skillet over medium-high heat. Lightly brush the halloum with olive oil and pomegranate molasses then grill for 1–2 minutes per side until golden and soft. Set aside on a plate to cool slightly.

Scatter the chilled watermelon over a large serving platter. Top with the grilled halloum and mint leaves, a drizzle of lemon juice and olive oil. Add a spoonful of pomegranate molasses for a touch of acidity and colour, if desired. Sprinkle with toasted sesame seeds, some freshly ground black pepper and a pinch of chilli flakes if you like.

Serve immediately, while the cheese is still warm and the watermelon cold. This salad is best enjoyed as a light lunch or mezza on hot days, with fresh Lebanese bread, olives, and a glass of arak or rose water. It pairs beautifully with grilled meats but is equally delicious on its own.

Notes...

Lebanese halloum is typically less salty than Cypriot halloumi. If using Cypriot cheese, soak in cold water for 15–20 minutes to reduce saltiness before grilling.

Always serve this salad fresh – it doesn't keep well once mixed.

Sawda Djej
سودة دجاج

Caramelised chicken livers with garlic,
lemon & pomegranate molasses
Serves 4–5

600g chicken livers, trimmed

5 tbsp extra virgin olive oil

6–7 garlic cloves, finely grated (don't
hold back – it carries the dish)

1¼ tsp fine sea salt, or to taste

1 tsp freshly ground black pepper

1½ tsp Baharat (Lebanese 7 spices)

3–4 tbsp pomegranate molasses

Juice of 1 lemon, or to taste

1 tbsp chopped fresh parsley, for garnish

Sawda Djej was one of those dishes Mum made with her eyes closed. The sizzle of garlic, the smell of frying livers, and that final swirl of dark, sweet-sour molasses always meant something warming was on the way. I remember dipping bread directly into the pan, my father reminding me to wipe it clean, fingers sticky with sauce, pickles on the side. It's a humble dish but in a Lebanese home, it means comfort and care, cooked with the hand of tradition.

Soak the chicken livers in cold water and lemon juice for 10 minutes to clean them and remove any bitterness, then rinse and pat completely dry.

Heat the olive oil in a wide sauté pan until shimmering. Add the garlic and stir gently until soft and fragrant but not browned. Add the livers and cook on medium-high heat, stirring occasionally, until browned on the outside but still tender inside – about 6–8 minutes. Season with the salt, black pepper, and Baharat.

Once the livers are mostly cooked through, pour in the pomegranate molasses and stir to coat, letting it reduce slightly and cling to the livers. Squeeze in the lemon juice and mix well, letting the sauce glaze the meat. Taste and adjust with more salt, lemon, or molasses if needed. Garnish with the fresh parsley.

Serve hot, straight from the pan, with pickles, lemon wedges, fresh mint, and lots of warm Lebanese khobez on the table.

Notes...

Don't skip the drying step — wet livers will steam instead of sear.

The flavour of pomegranate molasses varies – if it's very sweet, balance with extra lemon, and if very sour, reduce the amount of lemon juice slightly.

Pomegranate

Hindbeh b Zeit
هندبة بزيت

Sautéed wild dandelion greens with caramelised onions
Serves 4–5

800g dandelion greens or chicory, tough stems trimmed

100ml extra virgin olive oil

4 medium brown onions, halved and thinly sliced

7–8 large garlic cloves, finely grated

1 tbsp fine sea salt, or to taste

½ tsp freshly ground black pepper

Juice of 2 large lemons, or to taste

To serve
Olives

Lemon wedges

Warm Lebanese khobez

Hindbeh b Zeit was one of those dishes that marked the start of spring in my childhood. When the wild dandelion began to grow along the stone walls and in the fields, it quietly signalled a dish that came once a year, sometimes twice if rain was kind, and everyone waited for it like a gift from the earth. I remember my mum boiling and chopping the bitter greens, then topping them with sweet golden onions and generous amounts of lemon juice and olive oil. That was the taste of the land waking up after winter. Hindbeh was always eaten at room temperature with bread, olives, and long, quiet conversations around the table.

Rinse the greens thoroughly in several changes of cold water until there's no grit, then drain well. Bring a large pot of salted water to a boil and blanch the greens for 8–10 minutes until tender but still vibrant. Drain and then rinse in ice cold water to stop them cooking. Squeeze out all the excess water gently with your hands, then roughly chop the leaves and set aside.

In a wide sauté pan, heat 5 tablespoons of the olive oil and fry half of the sliced onions over medium-low heat with a pinch of salt until deeply golden and soft (around 20–25 minutes). Remove from the pan and set aside.

In the same pan with the remaining oil, fry the remaining onions with the garlic. Once fragrant and soft, stir in the chopped greens, season with the salt and pepper, and sauté gently for 5–6 minutes, just to combine and heat through.

Let the mixture cool slightly, then add the lemon juice and stir well. Transfer to a shallow dish, top generously with the caramelised onions, and serve at room temperature with olives, lemon wedges, and warm khobez on the side.

Notes...

Hindbeh tastes better after sitting for an hour once assembled, allowing the flavours to settle.

You can use frozen chicory if fresh is not in season or unavailable.

Mdardara
مدردرة

Hearty green lentils & rice with caramelised onions
Serves 4–5

300g green lentils

1.2–1.4L water

150ml olive oil

1kg (about 5–6) large brown onions, thinly sliced

1½ tsp ground cumin

1½ tsp fine sea salt, or to taste

½ tsp freshly ground black pepper

100g long grain rice, washed and drained

For the salatet banadoura
See the recipe for Ma'aale on page 63

To serve
Lemon wedges
Warm Lebanese khobez

Mdardara was one of those dishes that meant comfort when I was growing up. I still remember coming home from school in Beirut and before you even opened the door, you could smell the onions frying from the stairwell. The neighbours would always ask 'who's making mdardara today?' It wasn't just our home; in Békaa villages, in Akkar, in the South, this dish filled kitchens on simple days. My mother would cook it with green lentils and just a little rice, always to be served with salatet banadoura, a fresh tomato and cucumber salad, plenty of lemon and warm flatbread. Even now, that first bite brings back those cosy afternoons in our old house.

Wash the green lentils and place them in a large pot with the water. Bring to a boil, then lower the heat and simmer for 15–20 minutes, until the lentils are just tender but still holding their shape. Reserve the cooking water.

Meanwhile, in a large pan, heat the olive oil. Add the sliced onions and fry slowly over medium heat, stirring often, until deep golden brown and caramelised (about 25–30 minutes). Take your time – this step creates all the flavour. Remove about half the onions from the pan and set aside on a clean cloth or paper towels.

To the remaining onions in the pan, add the cumin, salt, and black pepper. Stir well. Add the cooked lentils and about 600ml of the reserved cooking water. Bring to a boil and then add the washed rice. Stir once, cover, and cook over low heat for 20–25 minutes, until the rice is tender and the water has been absorbed. Mdardara should be soft and comforting. If the mixture seems dry, add a little hot water.

Let it rest, covered, for 10 minutes while you prepare the salad, then fluff gently with a fork. Spoon the mdardara onto a large platter. Top generously with the reserved caramelised onions. Serve warm or at room temperature, alongside the traditional salad, warm Lebanese khobez, and extra lemon wedges if desired. In our house, this was always a simple, perfect, family lunch.

Notes...

Green lentils have a beautiful earthy flavour and hold their shape better than brown lentils. Using more lentils than rice is how mdardara is made correctly, home-style.

The caramelised onions must be very dark golden – take your time.

Classic Mezza
Untouched, uncompromised,
unmistakably Lebanese

There are dishes that change with time or evolve with trends, and then there are dishes you simply don't touch. The classic Lebanese mezza is sacred – not because of nostalgia, but because it was already perfect generations ago.

These are the staples that every Lebanese family knows by heart. Hummus made the right way, no 'twists' with avocado or beetroot. Mtabbal, whipped until silken the way my grandmother did, smoky with properly charred aubergines and good tahini. Baba Ghanouj that isn't confused with anything else – chunky, zesty, and alive with garlic.

Then there's falafel. Real Lebanese falafel, prepared with soaked chickpeas and fava beans, grounded with coriander and cumin, shaped and fried – not baked or air-fried – until deeply golden, crunchy on the outside, soft and airy on the inside. Break it apart with your hands, dip it in tarator, wrap it in warm khobez with pickles and radish, and that's a memory for life.

And don't even get me started on tabbouleh. The true queen of the mezza table. This isn't a bulgur salad, this is parsley in its full glory. Finely chopped, fresh and sharp, with juicy tomatoes, sweet onions, a hint of bulgur, and a dressing of lemon and olive oil that sings. There's no shortcut here. If it takes you twenty minutes to chop, then you're doing it right. It's not about speed – it's about care.

These aren't restaurant gimmicks or Instagram dishes. These are real recipes – the ones your mum makes on a Sunday, that your aunt brings to a picnic, that I still prepare the same way today. You'll see versions of these dishes in every cookbook, in every so-called Middle Eastern deli. But what makes this chapter different is that these recipes haven't been touched. Not modernised. Not diluted for foreign palates. They are as they should be, authentically Lebanese, and they are perfect this way, just like the hands that shaped them through generations before us.

This chapter is not just a celebration of flavour. It's a preservation of memory, of identity, of pride in what we've always done best – simple food, done properly.

Welcome to the table.

Hummus b' Thini
حمص بطحينة

The pride of Lebanon: silky-smooth,
tahini-rich & bright with lemon
Serves 4–5

250g dried chickpeas

1 tsp bicarbonate of soda (for soaking
and boiling)

1½ tsp fine sea salt, or to taste

2 small garlic cloves

2–4 small ice cubes (or use ice-cold
water)

200ml tahini

60ml fresh lemon juice (about 4 tbsp —
always fresh!)

2–4 tbsp chickpea cooking liquid (see
method)

Extra virgin olive oil, for serving

Paprika, cumin, parsley, or whole
chickpeas to garnish (optional)

For us Lebanese, hummus is more than a recipe, it's a part of who we are. It's not a garnish or a filler on the table; it's a dish that commands space, presence, and respect. Every Lebanese, no matter how humble or grand their kitchen, knows how to make hummus. And not just make it, perfect it. The balance of tahini, the sharpness of lemon, the right texture – it's a skill passed down like a sacred rite, from mother to daughter, from father to son. This hummus is silky, nutty, and deeply satisfying – the kind of dish that brings people to the table.

Start by rinsing the dried chickpeas under cold water. Soak overnight (no tinned chickpeas here, Habibi) in a large bowl with plenty of water and half the bicarbonate of soda – this softens the skins.

The next day, drain and rinse the soaked chickpeas. Place them in a large pot, cover with fresh water (about 10cm above the chickpeas), and add the remaining bicarbonate of soda. Bring to a boil, skimming off any foam that rises. Simmer gently for 1–1.5 hours, until the chickpeas are extremely soft – you should be able to mash one effortlessly between two fingers. Skim off any foam or skins floating on top during cooking.

Before draining, reserve 220–240ml of the cooking liquid (this is your secret weapon for extra flavour and creaminess). Drain the rest and set the chickpeas aside. While still warm, rub the chickpeas gently between your hands or in a bowl of cold water to remove some of the skins – this step is optional but creates that ultra-smooth finish. Set aside a small handful of whole chickpeas if you'd like to use them for garnish later.

Add the cooled chickpeas, salt, garlic cloves, and 2 ice cubes to a food processor. Blend into a fine paste for 2–3 minutes. Open the lid and scrape around the sides, then add the tahini and lemon juice and blend again for 2–3 minutes.

Now, slowly drizzle in 2-4 tablespoons of the reserved chickpea cooking liquid with the processor running, followed by 1 or 2 of the remaining ice cubes (or an equivalent amount of ice-cold water). Blend until the hummus becomes silky, fluffy, and pale in colour. The cold shock from the ice helps emulsify the tahini. Taste and adjust the seasoning. You're looking for balance – not too lemony, not too garlicky, with a mellow, nutty base from the tahini.

Chill for 30 minutes before serving if possible – this helps the flavours settle.

Spoon the hummus into a shallow bowl or plate, swirl the surface with the back of a spoon, and drizzle generously with extra virgin olive oil. Garnish with a few whole chickpeas, a sprinkle of paprika or cumin, and maybe a touch of fresh parsley. Serve with warm Lebanese khobez, fresh radishes, spring onions, or alongside grilled meat, falafel, or pickles. The best hummus tastes like your Teta's kitchen – simple, humble, and absolutely unforgettable.

Baba Ghanouj
بابا غنوج

Smoky aubergine salad
Serves 4–5

3 large aubergines (about 1.2kg), charred over flame or grill until blackened and soft (see method)

2 garlic cloves, finely grated

1 large ripe vine tomato, finely chopped

1 small bunch spring onions (about 100g), finely chopped

1 small bunch flat-leaf parsley (about 30g leaves), finely chopped

4 tbsp extra virgin olive oil

Juice of 1 lemon, or to taste

1 tsp fine sea salt, or to taste

Pinch of sumac or 1 tbsp pomegranate seeds (optional)

Poor Baba Ghanouj – this dish has been through an identity crisis in the West. You walk into a restaurant, order it with high hopes, and what lands on the table? Mtabbal. Creamy, tahini-loaded, delicious, yes – but not Baba Ghanouj. Let's set the record straight. The real Baba Ghanouj, the way we make it in Lebanon – especially in the villages – is a chunky aubergine salad. No tahini. No blender. Just smoky aubergine, fresh tomato, onion, lemon, parsley, garlic, and olive oil. It's bright, fresh, and alive with flavour. Growing up, we didn't need any excuse to make it – a few aubergines on the flame, neighbours dropping in unannounced, some bread on the side, and suddenly you had a mezza going. We called it a salad, but really it was a social event in a bowl.

Place the aubergines directly over a gas flame or grill and roast, turning frequently, until the skin is completely blackened and the flesh inside is soft and smoky. This will take about 10–15 minutes, depending on their size. Place in a bowl, cover, and let them steam for 10 minutes.

Peel off the charred skin, removing any burnt bits but leaving some char for flavour. Roughly chop the flesh by hand – do not use a blender – and place in a mixing bowl.

Add the grated garlic and finely chopped tomato, spring onion, and parsley to the aubergine. Drizzle in the olive oil and lemon juice, season with salt, then mix gently until just combined.

Taste and adjust the amount of lemon and salt to balance the flavours. Serve in a shallow dish, garnished with a drizzle of olive oil, a sprinkle of parsley, and a pinch of sumac or pomegranate seeds if you like. This is best eaten fresh, at room temperature, with khobez, and surrounded by people.

Notes...

The aubergine must be properly charred – that's where all the flavour comes from.

Never blend the aubergine – it's meant to be rustic and chunky, not smooth.

This dish is all about freshness. Eat within a few hours of making it.

Hummus Beiruti
حمص بيروتي

Smoky, herby, garlicky hummus – the
Beirut way
Serves 4–5

500g creamy hummus (see the recipe on
page 80)
5–6 confit garlic cloves (see below)
1 medium red chilli
1 small handful flat-leaf parsley (about
10g), picked, washed, and finely chopped
1 tsp smoked paprika
½ tsp Aleppo chilli flakes, or to taste
Fine sea salt, to taste
1 tbsp lemon juice (optional, to balance)
Extra virgin olive oil, to loosen if needed

For the garlic confit
5–6 garlic cloves, peeled
100ml olive oil

In Beirut, every café and home has its own version of
hummus, but Hummus Beiruti always stands out. It's the
cheekier cousin of the classic. I remember wandering
through Basta and Zarif in Beirut as a teen, hungry after
school, drawn into corners of smoky cafés by the smell of
lemony hummus mixed with sizzling garlic. This version
is my own spin – garlic confit for sweetness, charred chilli
for a gentle fire. The texture? Always smooth. The taste?
Bright, deep, and distinctly Beiruti.

First, make the garlic confit. Place all the peeled garlic cloves in a
small saucepan and cover with the olive oil. Simmer gently on the
lowest heat for about 25–30 minutes, or until the garlic is soft and
lightly golden. Let it cool in the oil. Mash 3–4 cloves for this recipe
and store the rest in a clean jar, covered with the oil, in the fridge for
up to 1 week.

Next, char the red chilli directly over a gas flame or under a hot grill,
turning until blackened all over. Place in a bowl and cover with a plate
or foil for 5 minutes to help loosen the skin. Peel off the charred skin,
remove the seeds, and finely chop half the chilli for this recipe. Keep
the other half aside to add extra heat if you like.

In a bowl, fold the mashed garlic confit, charred chilli, chopped
parsley, smoked paprika, and Aleppo chilli flakes into the creamy
hummus base. Season with salt, and lemon juice if needed. Add a
little olive oil to loosen the texture if it feels too thick.

Spoon the hummus into a serving dish, make a small swirl with the
back of a spoon, then garnish with a drizzle of olive oil, a sprinkle of
chopped parsley, and a touch more chilli or paprika. Serve with warm
khobez and let everyone dive in.

Notes...
Garlic confit brings depth without harshness
and a little goes a long way.

Adjust the chilli to your liking but keep the
balance. This is Beiruti, not fire alarm!

Make the mix up to 4 hours ahead, cover, and
keep at room temperature for best flavour.

Lebanese Muhammara

محمرة

Smoky, spicy roasted red pepper, walnut & olive oil dip

Serves 4–5

3 large red bell peppers (approx. 500g)

150g walnuts

2 tbsp (20g) fine breadcrumbs, preferably homemade or Lebanese-style kaak

2 tbsp (30ml) pomegranate molasses

2 large garlic cloves, finely grated

½ fresh long red chilli

1 tbsp red pepper paste

1 tsp Aleppo pepper or mild red chilli flakes

½ tsp ground cumin

1 tsp fine sea salt, or to taste

3 tbsp (45ml) extra virgin olive oil

Juice of ½ lemon

Muhammara was always that bold red bowl on the mezza table that caught the eye before anything else. Made with roasted peppers, walnuts, Aleppo pepper, and pomegranate molasses, it carried the warmth of the Levant and the spice of our southern mountains. My mother used to say it's the dip with a story: smoky, sweet, spicy, and deeply satisfying. We'd spread it on warm bread, always with a drizzle of olive oil, and it never lasted long.

Start by washing the red peppers thoroughly, drying them with a clean cloth, and placing them directly over a gas flame or charcoal grill, or under a hot grill. Let the skins char and blacken, turning with tongs until all sides are blistered and soft (this is where the smoky depth comes from — just like Teta did it). Once charred, transfer the peppers to a bowl and cover with cling film or a plate to let them steam for 10 minutes. This loosens the skin naturally. When cooled slightly, peel off the skins gently by hand (don't rinse under water, you'll lose the flavour), then remove the seeds and stalks from the flesh. Place this in a sieve or colander to cool further and drain off any excess liquid.

While the peppers cool, toast the walnuts lightly in a dry pan over medium heat for 2–3 minutes, just until fragrant — not burnt. This brings out their oil and deepens the flavour.

In a bowl or food processor, combine the roasted red pepper flesh, walnuts, breadcrumbs, pomegranate molasses, garlic, chilli, red pepper paste, Aleppo pepper, cumin, salt, and olive oil. Blend or mash together until you get a thick, coarse paste. Taste and adjust the seasoning. If you need a little more tang, add a squeeze of lemon juice. If the paste is too thick, drizzle in a bit more olive oil. Let it sit for 15–20 minutes at room temperature so the flavours marry.

Spoon the muhammara into a shallow dish, smooth it out, and finish with a generous drizzle of olive oil and a light dusting of Aleppo pepper or crushed walnuts on top.

Labneh Mtawwameh
لبنة متومة

Garlicky labneh dip
Serves 4–5

400g labneh (thick strained yoghurt)

1–2 garlic cloves, finely grated

2 tbsp extra virgin olive oil, plus extra for drizzling

1½ tsp fine sea salt, or to taste

 Pinch of za'atar, for garnish

This was the dip always on the breakfast table: thick, garlicky, and perfect with warm bread. My mother used to say, 'if you're eating labneh mtawwameh, everyone will know it.' I'd spread it in a warm Lebanese flatbread with cucumber and olives before running out the door. Simple, strong, and full of childhood flavour.

In a mixing bowl, combine the labneh with the garlic, olive oil, and salt. Mix well until smooth and creamy. Taste and adjust the garlic and seasoning – it should be tangy with a gentle kick of garlic, not overpowering.

Spoon into a serving bowl, swirl the top with the back of a spoon, drizzle with a little olive oil, and garnish with a sprinkle of za'atar if desired.

Mtabbal Batenjen
متبل باذنجان

Creamy, garlicky, smoky: the real Lebanese mtabbal
Serves 4–5

700–800g aubergines (about 2 large ones)

100g good quality Lebanese tahini

2 garlic cloves, finely grated

3 tbsp fresh lemon juice (approx. 45ml)

2 tsp fine sea salt, or to taste

2 tbsp extra virgin olive oil, for drizzling

Fresh chopped parsley, for garnish

Sprinkle of pomegranate seeds, for decoration

Mtabbal was the taste of every family gathering for me growing up – smoky, tangy, and always made by hand. I remember sitting on the floor watching my mum mash the aubergine with a fork – no blender, just love.

Start by charring the whole aubergines directly over an open gas flame or charcoal grill, turning occasionally until the skin is fully blackened and blistered and the inside is completely soft. This should take about 10–15 minutes depending on their size. If you don't have an open flame, the grill (broiler) in your oven works well too; just be sure to rotate them for even charring. Once cooked, place the aubergines in a bowl and cover with foil or cling film to steam slightly for 5–10 minutes (this makes peeling easier).

Once cool enough to handle, peel away the burnt skin carefully, keeping as much of the soft smoky flesh as possible, and avoid rinsing it with water so you don't lose that deep flavour. Place the flesh in a sieve or colander and let any liquid drain for 10–15 minutes.

For a more rustic texture, mash the aubergine flesh with a fork. For a smoother dip, pulse it briefly in the processor. Add the tahini, garlic, lemon juice, and salt, then mix or blend until creamy and well combined. Taste and adjust the seasoning if needed.

Spoon the mtabbal into a shallow bowl, use the back of a spoon to create a little swirl, and drizzle with the extra virgin olive oil. Finish with the chopped parsley and pomegranate seeds for colour. Serve with warm Lebanese khobez for dipping.

Saida-Style Falafel
فلافل صيدا بالفول

The taste of Saida's souk, freshly fried
and drizzled with tahini
Serves 4–5

300g dried chickpeas

100g dried broad beans

1 medium onion, roughly chopped
(approx. 100g)

5–6 large garlic cloves, finely grated
(approx. 25g)

1 bunch fresh coriander, roughly chopped
(approx. 80g)

1 small bunch fresh dill, roughly chopped

1 tsp ground cumin

1 tsp ground coriander

1½ tsp fine sea salt

½ tsp freshly ground black pepper

1–2 tsp baking powder

1 tsp bicarbonate of soda

50g sesame seeds

Rapeseed oil, for frying (approx. 500ml)

Notes...

The broad beans give these falafel a lighter,
smoother texture, which is one of the
distinctive features of Saida's version. This
combination makes the falafel feel softer and
airier than the typical chickpea-only version.

Chill the mixture thoroughly before shaping.
This helps the falafel hold together and
prevents them from falling apart during
frying.

If you want to add a kick, you can mix in a
small pinch of chilli flakes or even a small
chopped green chilli along with the spices.

The bicarbonate of soda and baking powder
are essential in making this falafel light and
fluffy. They help to create that perfect crispy
exterior with a soft, airy interior.

In Saida, falafel isn't just food, it's an experience that
brings people together. I remember as a child, my family
and I would visit the southern coastal city, and there was
always a stop for falafel. The air was filled with the scent of
them. We'd stand outside the shop with a falafel sandwiché
in one hand and a handful of chilli pickles in the other.
As the tarator (tahini sauce) dripped down our fingers,
we'd laugh, talk, and share that moment of pure joy. The
falafel was crispy on the outside, tender on the inside, and
wrapped in warm khobez. What made it unforgettable was
the way it tied us to the city, the culture, and even strangers
who were also savouring the same humble delight. No
matter how busy life got, that simple sandwich was always a
reason to stop and enjoy the moment.

In a large bowl, soak both the chickpeas and broad beans in plenty of
water overnight (about 12–18 hours). Drain and rinse them well.

To prepare the falafel mixture, place the soaked chickpeas, broad
beans, onion, garlic, coriander, and dill into a food processor. Pulse
until the mixture is coarsely ground. It should still have a bit of
texture but should come together when you shape it. If the mixture is
too wet, strain it for few minutes.

Add the cumin, coriander, salt, and black pepper to the falafel
mixture. Sprinkle in the baking powder and bicarbonate of soda, then
pulse again to combine all the ingredients or transfer into a large bowl
and mix by hand.

Cover the mixture with a kitchen towel and refrigerate it for 1 hour.
This resting period allows the flavours to meld and helps the mixture
firm up for easier shaping.

After resting, wet your hands and shape the mixture into small balls
or patties (about the size of a small lime). Be careful not to overpack
the mixture, as the falafel should be light and airy inside. Dip each
falafel in the sesame seeds on one side only.

Pour the oil into a frying pan or wok, ensuring it's deep enough to
submerge the falafel, and heat to 180°C. Test the temperature by
dropping a small piece of the falafel mixture into the oil – it should
sizzle and rise to the surface.

Fry the falafel in batches, being careful not to overcrowd the pan.
Fry each batch for 4–5 minutes, or until the falafel are golden brown
and crispy on all sides. Use a slotted spoon to remove them from the
oil and place them on paper towels to drain any excess oil. Serve the
falafel immediately, while still hot and crispy, with warm khobez.

Stuff your falafel sandwiches with pickled turnips, sliced tomato,
slices of radish, and mint leaves, then drizzle generously with tarator
(see page 202) for the true taste of Saida's falafel shops.

Khadija's Tabbouleh
تبولة

The beginning of every gathering: my mum's tabbouleh
Serves 4–5

2 large bunches fresh flat-leaf parsley leaves (approx. 150g)

1 small bunch fresh mint leaves (approx. 25g)

3–4 ripe medium vine tomatoes, finely chopped (approx. 400g)

3–4 spring onions, very finely chopped

1 tbsp fine brown burghul (about 15g)

5–6 tbsp freshly squeezed lemon juice (about 75ml)

4–5 tbsp extra virgin olive oil (about 75ml)

1 tbsp fine sea salt, or to taste

1 tsp Baharat (Lebanese 7 spices)

4–5 romaine lettuce leaves

Tabbouleh is the soul of our mezza. You can have ten dishes on the table – grilled meats, kibbeh, fatteh – but if the tabbouleh is missing, something feels wrong. It's not a side dish – it's the dish that brings brightness, freshness, life. In our culture, tabbouleh is made to be eaten together, slowly, with conversation. You take a crisp lettuce leaf, scoop some tabbouleh into it, fold it by hand (no cutlery needed) and eat. Every family, every region, has its own touch: more lemon, more mint, more tomatoes. But the core remains the same – green, sharp, alive. This version is just like Khadija would make.

Always start by washing the parsley and mint thoroughly. Soak them in cold water with a splash of vinegar, rinse 2–3 times, and drain well. Spread the herbs on a clean cloth or place them in a salad spinner to dry fully. Once dry, chop the herbs finely. The chopping must be by hand with a sharp knife, never a processor. It takes time, but it's worth it. The herbs should be fine, fluffy, and full of aroma.

The tomatoes must be ripe but firm, juicy but not watery, and always chopped into very small pieces (around 5–7mm). If they're too juicy, let them sit in a sieve briefly.

In a large bowl, combine the chopped parsley, mint, tomatoes, spring onion, and burghul. Add the lemon juice, olive oil, salt, and Baharat. Mix gently but thoroughly; the tabbouleh should be well combined, tangy, and fresh — not oily or watery. Taste and adjust the salt or lemon to your liking.

Serve fresh and slightly chilled, ideally within 1–2 hours of making, with the lettuce leaves.

Fatayer b'Sbenegh
فطاير سبانخ

Golden pastry parcels with tangy spinach
& onion filling

Serves 4–5 | Makes about 12 medium
fatayer

For the dough

500g strong plain flour

1 tsp sugar

1 tsp fine sea salt

7g dried instant yeast

4–5 tbsp extra virgin olive oil, plus extra
for brushing

300ml lukewarm water, plus 1–2 tbsp if
needed

3–4 tbsp lukewarm milk (for softer
dough)

For the filling

300g fresh spinach, washed thoroughly,
drained, and finely chopped

2 small brown onions, finely diced

Juice of 2 large lemons

15–20ml extra virgin olive oil

1 tbsp pomegranate molasses

2 tbsp sumac

½ tbsp fine sea salt, or to taste

¼ tsp freshly ground black pepper, or to
taste

Fatayer b'Sbenegh isn't just a recipe, it's a full day in
our home. I remember clearly how my mother and our
neighbour upstairs, Em Ali, would plan it days in advance.
They'd agree on the morning, sometimes at our place,
sometimes at hers. The sound of early knocks on the door,
the scent of chopped onions, the dough resting under
cotton towels all meant one thing: fatayer day had begun.

The two of them worked like clockwork, one preparing the
spinach and sumac filling, the other shaping the dough.
They weren't just making enough for the family, but for
the neighbours too. The entire building would fill with the
smell of baking pastries, lemon, and olive oil. The stairs
echoed with laughter, shouted instructions, and the warmth
of something more than food – our community.

To prepare the dough

In the bowl of a stand mixer with a dough hook, combine the flour,
sugar, and salt. Start mixing on low speed while gradually pouring in
the yeast and liquids. Let the dough hook knead the mixture for about
6–8 minutes until a smooth, elastic, and slightly tacky dough forms. If
the dough feels a bit stiff, add 1–2 more tablespoons of warm water.

Once the dough is smooth, remove it from the mixer, shape into a
ball, and lightly oil the surface. Return it to the bowl, cover with a
clean kitchen towel, and leave in a warm place to rise for about 1
hour, or until doubled in size.

To prepare the filling

Place the chopped spinach in a bowl and sprinkle with a bit of salt. Let
it sit for 10–15 minutes to release moisture, then squeeze it well with
your hands and discard the liquid. Add the finely diced onions, lemon
juice, olive oil, pomegranate molasses, sumac, salt, and black pepper.
Mix well and taste – it should be tangy and fresh.

To assemble and bake the fatayer

Preheat your oven to 200°C (180°C fan). Line a baking tray with
parchment paper. Divide the dough into equal balls of about 40–50g
each. Roll out each ball into a thin circle about 8–10cm in diameter.
Place 1 tablespoon of filling in the centre of the circle, then bring up
the edges of the dough towards the middle on three sides and pinch
them together, creating a triangular shape and enclosing the filling.

Place the prepared fatayer on the lined tray and brush them lightly all
over with olive oil. Bake for 12–15 minutes in the preheated oven until
golden on the bottom and lightly coloured on top. If you would like
them more golden, you can pop them under a hot grill for a minute at
the end.

Let the fatayer cool slightly and then serve warm, or at room
temperature, with fresh lemon wedges.

Salatet Shamandar
سلطة الشمندر

Sweet, salty, crunchy beetroot, feta &
walnut salad
Serves 4–5

500g (2–3 medium) red beetroots

40g fresh purslane (baa'leh)

60g walnuts

100g Greek-style feta cheese, cubed or
crumbled

2 spring onions, thinly sliced, green and
white parts

3 tbsp extra virgin olive oil

2 tbsp freshly squeezed lemon juice

1 tsp fine sea salt, or to taste

¼ tsp freshly ground black pepper

1 tsp pomegranate molasses (optional)

2 tbsp fresh pomegranate seeds, for
garnish

This salad reminds me of summers in the mountains of Lebanon, where the air was cool, the soil was red, and root vegetables thrived. My grandmother would boil the beets early in the morning and leave them to cool on the marble counter while she picked fresh baa'leh (purslane) from the garden. We ate it cold, with creamy feta – we call it Bélgharé in Lebanon – from the local dairy and a drizzle of olive oil pressed just days before. It's a northern village dish: fresh, earthy, and full of texture, just like the land it comes from.

Start by scrubbing the beetroots under cold water, using a vegetable brush to remove all soil. Place them whole (skin on) into a large pot of cold water. Bring to a boil, then simmer gently for 35–45 minutes, or until tender when pierced with a knife. Drain and set aside to cool. Once cool enough to handle, slip off the skins with your hands or a small knife and slice into rounds.

While the beets are boiling, wash the purslane thoroughly in cold water with a splash of white vinegar. Let it soak for a few minutes to remove any grit, then rinse twice more and spin or pat completely dry. Pick the leaves and tender stems only.

Lightly toast the walnuts in a dry pan over medium heat for 3–4 minutes until fragrant. Set aside to cool, then roughly chop.

In a large bowl, combine the sliced beetroot, purslane, walnuts, feta, and spring onions. Drizzle with the olive oil and lemon juice. Season with salt and black pepper. If using, add a light drizzle of pomegranate molasses for brightness and depth. Toss gently until the ingredients are just coated, taking care not to break up the feta too much.

Transfer to a serving dish and top with pomegranate seeds for colour and freshness. Serve the salad cold or at room temperature as part of a mezza spread, or alongside grilled lamb, chicken, or even a simple mujaddara.

Batata Harra
بطاطا حرّة

Crunchy potatoes sizzling with garlic,
coriander & chilli
Serves 4–5

800g Maris Piper or chipping potatoes

30g fresh coriander leaves and stems

500ml rapeseed oil, for frying

5 tbsp extra virgin olive oil

8 garlic cloves, finely grated

2 tsp Aleppo chilli flakes, or to taste

1½ tsp fine sea salt, or to taste

1 tsp ground cumin

Juice of ½ lemon

Every Friday night, this dish reminded me that we didn't need much to feel rich. The whole house smelled like fried garlic and fresh herbs. My mum made it with just a few ingredients, but it brought the whole family around the table. It was always warm, always spicy, and full of love.

Start by thoroughly washing the potatoes under cold running water. Peel them, cut into even 1–1.5cm cubes, then place in a bowl of fresh cold water. Soak them for 10–15 minutes to remove excess starch, which will help them crisp up and prevent sticking. After soaking, rinse them again, then spread out on a clean kitchen towel or paper towels. Pat completely dry, as any moisture left on the surface will make the oil splatter and prevent crisping.

Next, wash the coriander leaves and stems in a bowl of cold water with a splash of vinegar or a pinch of salt. Swish well to remove any grit or soil. Rinse under fresh water twice, then dry thoroughly using a salad spinner or clean towel. Set aside and chop finely, stems included as they carry deep flavour.

Heat the rapeseed oil in a deep pot or pan over medium-high heat. When the oil is hot, fry the potatoes in batches. Do not overcrowd the pan. Fry until golden and crispy on the outside and soft on the inside, about 7–9 minutes per batch. Remove with a slotted spoon and set them on a paper towel-lined tray to drain any excess oil.

In a wide sauté pan, warm the olive oil over medium heat. Add the garlic and stir gently for just 15–20 seconds. Don't let it brown. Immediately add the chopped coriander and let it sizzle until aromatic, between 30 seconds and 1 minute.

Add the fried potatoes to the garlic and coriander mix. Season with the chilli flakes, salt, and cumin. Toss everything together for a few minutes so that every cube of potato is fully coated with flavour.
To finish, squeeze in the lemon juice, give everything one final toss, and remove from the heat. Serve warm or at room temperature with Lebanese khobez and laban. A perfect mezza dish or side alongside grilled meats or fish.

Salatet Fattoush
فتوش

Lebanon's signature salad: colourful
vegetables, crisp khobez & bright sumac
Serves 4–5

1–2 large romaine lettuces, washed and
torn by hand

2 medium, firm, ripe vine tomatoes, cut
into 1.5–2cm cubes

1–2 medium cucumbers, diced (use baby
Lebanese cucumbers if possible)

1 small green bell pepper, deseeded
and diced

5–6 radishes, thinly sliced

2 spring onions or ½ small red onion,
finely chopped

Handful of fresh flat-leaf parsley, roughly
chopped

Handful of fresh mint leaves, roughly
chopped

2 small Lebanese flatbreads

1 tbsp sumac

3–4 tbsp extra virgin olive oil

A few leaves of fresh purslane (optional,
if available)

For the dressing
(Tarator el Fattoush)

5 tbsp extra virgin olive oil (60ml)

2 tbsp fresh lemon juice (30ml)

1 tbsp grape vinegar or apple cider
vinegar (15ml)

1 large garlic clove, finely grated

1 tbsp sumac

1½ tsp fine sea salt, or to taste

1 tbsp pomegranate molasses (optional)

During summer and Ramadan, there was always a big bowl
of fattoush on the table – crunchy bread, lemony dressing,
and the scent of mint in the air. As my Teta used to say, if
it's not sharp and fresh, it's not fattoush. This is the way it's
done at home.

First, wash all the vegetables properly. Soak the lettuce and herbs in
cold water with a splash of vinegar for a few minutes, rinse, and dry
well using a clean towel or spinner. Crunch and freshness are key –
soggy leaves have no place in fattoush. Chop everything just before
serving to keep it fresh. The tomatoes shouldn't be too fine, so they
hold their shape and don't turn watery in the salad.

Cut the flatbreads into small squares (about 2cm) and either fry in
rapeseed oil or bake in the oven until golden and crunchy (but fried is
traditional). Sprinkle them with the sumac and drizzle with olive oil.

In a small bowl, make the dressing by whisking all the ingredients
together until well combined. Taste and adjust the seasoning if
needed – the dressing should be punchy, lemony, and a little garlicky.
If you're using pomegranate molasses for a touch of sweetness, just a
drizzle will round it off.

Immediately before serving, toss all the vegetables and herbs in a
large bowl. Pour over the dressing and toss well to coat. Add the
crispy bread last, folding it in gently so it doesn't get soggy. Serve
immediately.

Salatet l'Batata
سلطة البطاطا

Fluffy potatoes dressed in lemon, olive oil & pomegranate

Serves 4–5

800g waxy potatoes, such as Jersey Royals or Charlotte

20g fresh flat-leaf parsley

20g fresh mint leaves

2 spring onions

40g pitted black or green olives

80g fresh pomegranate seeds (about ½ pomegranate)

4 tbsp freshly squeezed lemon juice (about 2 medium lemons)

60ml extra virgin olive oil

3 garlic cloves, finely grated

1½ tsp fine sea salt, or to taste

1 tsp freshly ground black pepper

2 tbsp pomegranate molasses

This salad was always part of our Sunday table when I was growing up in Beirut. My mum made it early in the morning so the garlic, lemon, and olive oil could soak into the warm potatoes. When pomegranates were in season, she'd toss in the seeds for colour and sweetness. We never needed mayonnaise, just fresh herbs and good olive oil.

Start by scrubbing the potatoes well under cold running water. Place them whole (skins on) in a deep pot, cover with cold water, and add a pinch of salt. Bring to a boil, then reduce to a simmer and cook until fork-tender, about 20–25 minutes. You should be able to pierce them easily, but they should not fall apart.

While the potatoes cook, wash the parsley and mint thoroughly in a bowl of cold water with a splash of white vinegar or a pinch of salt. Swish the leaves to remove any dirt, drain, and rinse twice more under cold water. Dry completely using a clean towel or salad spinner, then finely chop and set aside.

Rinse and slice the spring onions thinly, using both the green and white parts. Cut the olives into halves or small pieces. If using a fresh pomegranate, slice it open and gently remove the seeds, discarding the bitter membrane.

Once the potatoes are cooked, drain and allow them to cool slightly. While still warm (but not hot), peel by hand or with a small knife. Cut into quarters and place in a large bowl. Add the lemon juice, olive oil, garlic, salt, and pepper. Gently fold to coat all the cubes while the potatoes are still warm, allowing them to absorb the dressing. Add the chopped herbs, spring onions, olives, and pomegranate seeds. Mix again gently, just until combined, then drizzle with the pomegranate molasses.

Allow the salad to sit at room temperature for 20–30 minutes before serving. Serve at room temperature as part of a mezza, alongside grilled chicken, kafta, or fish – or simply enjoy by itself.

Arayes
عرايس

Grilled Lebanese khobez stuffed with
spiced minced lamb
Serves 4–5

100g lean beef mince

400g minced lamb shoulder (20% fat)

1 small brown onion, very finely chopped

Handful of flat-leaf parsley, washed, dried
thoroughly and finely chopped (approx.
20g)

1½ tsp Baharat (Lebanese 7 spices)

1½ tsp fine sea salt, or to taste

½ tsp freshly ground black pepper

¼ tsp grated nutmeg

4–5 large khobez (ideally fresh from a
Middle Eastern store)

2–3 tbsp light olive oil or rapeseed oil, for
brushing

1 tbsp pomegranate molasses

Arayes is more than a street food. It's the call of summer
evenings, when the scent of sizzling meat and toasted
bread fills the neighbourhood just as the sun dips behind
the hills. Khadija's hands, moving fast between the bowl
of spiced kafta and the stack of warm khobez, are a scene
engraved in my memory. In Lebanon, arayes is eaten hot off
the grill with laban and pickled turnips or wrapped in foil
for road trips down the coast – the kind of food that makes
people pause and smile mid-bite.

To prepare the kafta mixture

In a clean mixing bowl, combine the beef and lamb mince with the
chopped onion and parsley. Add the Baharat, salt, black pepper, and
nutmeg. Using your hand, mix the ingredients thoroughly for about
2–3 minutes until the meat becomes slightly sticky. This helps to bind
everything together and gives the kafta its traditional texture. Cover
and refrigerate for 15–20 minutes while you prepare the bread and
heat the grill.

To assemble and cook the arayes

Cut the khobez into halves or quarters, depending on their size.
Gently open each piece to form a pocket. Using a spoon or clean
hands, spread a thin layer of the kafta mixture inside each pocket
(about 1 heaped tablespoon), pressing it evenly into the bread. The
meat layer should be no thicker than 0.5cm. Close the pocket gently
and brush both sides with a little oil.

On a preheated grill pan, sandwich press, or outdoor barbecue, cook
the arayes on medium heat for 3–4 minutes on each side, pressing
lightly, until the bread is golden and crisp and the meat is fully
cooked. If you prefer to use your oven, you can bake the arayes on
a tray at 220°C (200°C fan) for 12–15 minutes, flipping them over
halfway through, and then finish under the grill for 2–3 minutes to
crisp them up.

Serve hot, drizzled with pomegranate molasses and enjoyed
alongside laban, pickles, or a cucumber and mint salad. You can also
wrap them in foil for picnic-style presentation, just like they do at
Beirut gas station snack bars!

Zeitoun Mchakkal
زيتون مشكل

Lebanese marinated green & black olives
Serves 4–5 with mezza

250g green olives (preferably cracked or whole with pit)

250g black olives (preferably oil-cured or wrinkled-style)

4 tbsp extra virgin olive oil (the good stuff!)

1 large lemon, zested and juiced

1 garlic clove, finely grated

½ bunch za'atar or regular thyme leaves

1 small fresh chilli, thinly sliced (optional)

Freshly ground black pepper, to taste

There is no Lebanese table, breakfast, lunch, or mezza without a small bowl of olives. Always there, always full, always passed around with love. For us, olives are not just a side. They're part of our identity, our land, our seasons. From the north to the south, olive trees stand tall, some hundreds of years old, rooted in the soil like family. My childhood memories are full of olive harvests, Teta with her basket, hands dark from sorting, the smell of brine in the kitchen.

Whether it's the deep black ones from the south, soft and wrinkled, or the firm, green, bitter olives cracked and cured at home – each bite carries a story. Some are packed with garlic and chilli, others just with salt and lemon. They're eaten with bread and labneh, next to kibbeh nayyeh, or simply one by one with a sip of arak on a lazy Sunday.

In every Lebanese home, there's always a jar of olives, homemade or from a trusted village. They're passed down like secrets. And when someone visits, we never forget to offer a few. These marinated olives are simple, rustic and bursting with bold Levantine flavour – just make sure you have a good olive oil, and maybe your Teta's wooden spoon.

If your olives are very salty (especially cured black ones), give them a quick rinse under cold water and drain well. You don't want to wash the flavour away, just mellow the saltiness if needed. Pat dry with a kitchen towel.

In a medium mixing bowl, combine the olive oil, lemon zest, lemon juice, garlic, thyme, chilli (if using), and a good grind of black pepper. Add the olives and toss everything together gently but thoroughly, making sure every olive gets coated in that garlicky, herby goodness.

Let the olives sit at room temperature for at least 30 minutes before serving – or, even better, cover and refrigerate for a few hours so the flavours really marry. Bring them back to room temperature before serving, as cold olive oil can dull the flavours.

Serve in a small shallow bowl as part of a mezza with warm Lebanese flatbread, labné, and fresh vegetables. Don't forget to put a little bowl on the side for pits – Lebanese table manners!

Tabkha

The warmth and comfort
of a Lebanese family table

When people outside Lebanon think of our food, they often picture mezza
– colourful plates of hummus, mtabbal, kibbé, tabbouleh, fatteh. While
mezza is beautiful, what truly feeds the Lebanese family, what fills the
house with comfort and warmth, is something humbler and more honest.

Tabkha simply means 'a cooked dish', which might be a stew, a pot of
beans, a braised vegetable, or a slow-simmered plate of comfort food. This
is the food of the Lebanese family table. It is what mothers cook for their
children when they come home from school. It is what fathers look
forward to when they return from work. It is what we eat together at
lunch, seated at the table with fresh bread, salad, and steaming rice.

In my house, the day was built around the tabkha. My mother would start
early in the morning. She soaked the beans, peeled the vegetables,
chopped the onions and garlic, laid everything out on the kitchen counter.
You could hear onions sizzling in olive oil, the soft bubbling of a pot on
the stove. The house would begin to fill with the scent of cumin or
cinnamon or coriander, depending on what was cooking that day. As a
boy, I would come home from school and know what was for lunch before
I even opened the door, just from the aroma in the stairwell.

Tabkha is not a recipe you follow with a stopwatch. It takes time, and care.
The onions must cook slowly until sweet; the garlic added at just the right
moment. The broth must be tasted, adjusted, balanced. My mother always
said 'you cook tabkha with your eyes, your hands, and your heart.'

It is also deeply seasonal. Winter meant hearty dishes like fasoulia
b'lahmé, mloukhieh, rez w djej, and bazella. In summer, we'd enjoy
lighter plates of loubieh b'zeit or mdardara with laban. The vegetables
came from the market or relatives' gardens. Nothing was wasted.

Every family in Lebanon has its own way of preparing these cooked dishes.
This is what makes tabkha so alive. It is not fixed; it breathes with each
family's own tastes and traditions. And always, it is served with pride. The
pot comes to the table, the rice is fluffed, the salad is crisp, the bread is
warm. Everyone eats together. It is not food for guests, it is food for the
family. This is what my children will remember, just as I remember the
tabkha of my mother and my teta. This is how our food lives on.

Freekeh b'Lahmé
فريكة باللحمة

Smoky roasted green wheat with lamb,
sultanas & toasted nuts

Serves 4–5

For the lamb and broth

60–80ml olive oil

1.5kg bone-in lamb shoulder, cut into
200–250g chunks

3–3.5L cold water

2 large brown onions (about 400g),
halved

2 bay leaves

1 cinnamon stick

6–8 whole cardamom pods

1 tsp whole black peppercorns

1½ tsp fine sea salt

For the freekeh

500g whole freekeh

3 tbsp olive oil

4 tbsp butter or samneh

1 medium brown onion, finely diced

5 garlic cloves, finely grated

100g golden sultanas

2½ tsp Baharat (Lebanese 7 spices)

1½ tsp fine sea salt, or to taste

½ tsp freshly ground black pepper

1–1.2L hot lamb broth (see above)

4 tbsp almonds, whole or halved

4 tbsp pine nuts

2 tbsp pistachios

Notes...

Bone-in lamb shoulder always gives the best
flavour.

Do not skip toasting the freekeh – this brings
out its smoky flavour.

The freekeh must be fluffy – never mushy.

Freekeh is one of the oldest dishes in our cuisine. It dates
back to ancient times, when farmers would harvest green
wheat, dry it over wood fires, and rub it to remove the
husk – which is why it's called freekeh, from the word
farak (to rub). It was a dish of the land, full of nutrients,
high in fibre and protein, designed to feed large families.
I remember my mother buying it from the old souks in
Beirut – she always chose the greenest, smokiest grains.
In Békaa and Zahlé, they cook it in a rustic style, while in
Beirut you find the more refined version with bone-in lamb
shoulder and toasted nuts. Every house has its way –but
the scent of freekeh toasting in butter is one that brings
everyone to the table.

To prepare the lamb and broth

Heat the oil in a large pan over medium heat. Add the lamb and
brown well on all sides, then cover with the cold water and bring to
a boil. Skim off any foam that forms on the surface and when the
water is clear, add the remaining ingredients. Lower the heat, cover
and simmer for 2–2.5 hours until the lamb is tender. Check every 30
minutes. Once done, remove the chunks of lamb and set aside. Strain
and reserve the broth, keeping it hot.

To prepare the freekeh

While the lamb is cooking, wash the freekeh thoroughly, rinsing the
grains 3 or 4 times until the water runs clear. Pick out any dark pieces
or stones. Drain well.

In a large heavy pot, heat the olive oil with half of the butter or
samneh. Add the onion and garlic and cook for 3–4 minutes until soft
and golden, then add the freekeh and stir gently for 5–7 minutes until
fragrant and lightly nutty. Stir in the golden sultanas.

Add the Baharat, salt, and black pepper to the pot and stir well. Add
approximately 1–1.2 litres of the reserved hot broth – enough to
cover the freekeh by 1 or 2cm. Bring to a boil, cover, lower the heat,
and simmer gently for 20–25 minutes, until the freekeh is tender
and the broth has been absorbed. The grains should stay fluffy and
separate, with a smoky aroma. Rest the freekeh, covered, for 10
minutes, then fluff gently with a fork.

In a small pan, heat the remaining butter or samneh and toast the
almonds, pine nuts and pistachios until golden. Watch carefully
to make sure the nuts don't burn. Tip them onto a plate lined with
kitchen paper and leave to cool slightly.

Arrange the fluffy freekeh on a large platter. Place the lamb pieces
on top or on the side. Scatter the toasted nuts generously over the
freekeh. In our house, we always poured a little extra broth over the
platter too – pure comfort.

Bemieh b'Lahmé
بامية باللحمة

Slow-cooked baby okra & lamb stew
Serves 4–5

60–80ml olive oil

600g bone-in lamb shoulder, cut into
150–200g chunks, or lamb ribs

1 medium brown onion (about 200g),
finely chopped

8 garlic cloves, finely grated

3 tbsp tomato paste

5 large ripe tomatoes (about 750g),
peeled and finely chopped or grated

1 large bunch fresh coriander, washed
and finely chopped

1 tbsp fine sea salt, or to taste

½ tsp freshly ground black pepper

1 tbsp Baharat (Lebanese 7 spices)

1.5–2L water

800g fresh or good quality frozen small
bemieh (okra)

1 tbsp samneh (ghee)

Bemieh b'lahmé is a dish you'll find from the mountains of the Chouf to the coastal cities of Saida and Tyre. Each family has their own way of preparing the stew. In the South, where bemieh (okra) is grown in abundance, they prefer a lighter, more garlicky version, often cooked with smaller pods and a generous squeeze of lemon at the table. In the mountains, the dish tends to be richer, with more tomato and a deeper broth. In Beirut, it is usually made with beef, while in the South and the Békaa, lamb is the meat of choice. In our house, my mother followed the Southern style – light, fresh, and always with plenty of coriander. She would seek out the smallest bemieh she could find in the market and when they weren't in season, she used frozen, which gives excellent results.

Heat the olive oil in a large pot over medium heat. Add the lamb and brown well on all sides. Add the finely chopped onion and sauté until soft and golden, then add the garlic and sauté gently for a minute until fragrant.

Add the tomato paste and stir well for 2 minutes, coating the meat and onions. Now add the fresh tomatoes. Cook gently for about 5–7 minutes, until the tomatoes have softened and the sauce begins to come together.

Add the chopped coriander directly into the pot. Stir to combine it with the tomato mixture and cook gently for a minute or two, allowing the coriander to release its aroma into the sauce.

Add the salt, black pepper, and Baharat, then pour in the water. Stir and bring to a gentle boil, skimming off any foam if needed.

Lower the heat and simmer gently, covered, for about 1.5–2 hours, stirring occasionally. The meat should be tender and the broth rich and well-flavoured.

If using fresh bemieh, wash and dry them well, then trim off the stalks without piercing the pods. If using frozen bemieh, rinse under cold water to remove any ice and drain well.

In a shallow frying pan, heat the samneh (you can use olive oil instead if you prefer) and sauté the bemieh for 2–3 minutes, then add it to the pot of stew. Stir very gently to avoid breaking the pods. Simmer uncovered for about 20–25 minutes, until the bemieh is tender and has absorbed the flavours of the sauce.

Taste and adjust the seasoning as needed. The stew should have a rich tomato broth, tender meat, and soft but whole bemieh.

Serve hot alongside Lebanese rice with vermicelli, warm khobez, fresh radishes, chilli pickles, and lemon wedges.

Djej b'Sayniyeh
دجاج بالصينية

Tray-baked chicken with potatoes, garlic, lemon & coriander
Serves 4–5

1 whole chicken (about 1.4–1.6kg), cut into 6–8 pieces, skin on

16 large garlic cloves, finely grated

250ml freshly squeezed lemon juice

150ml olive oil

1½ tsp fine sea salt, or to taste

1 tsp freshly ground black pepper

1½ tsp Baharat (Lebanese 7 spices)

½ tsp ground coriander

½ tsp ground turmeric

800g Maris Piper or chipping potatoes, peeled and sliced into 1–1.5cm rounds

1 large bunch fresh coriander (about 80g), washed, picked and finely chopped

200ml water

In South Lebanon, this dish was always a weekend favourite. One big tray in the middle of the table, the scent of garlic and lemon filling the house, and everyone fighting over the crispiest piece of potato. My mother would start prepping it early in the day, seasoning every layer by hand, making sure nothing was dry or bland. It was the kind of meal that brought the neighbours in, uninvited but always welcome – you just had to follow your nose.

Rinse the chicken pieces thoroughly under cold water and pat them dry with kitchen paper. In a bowl, toss them with half the grated garlic, half the lemon juice, half the olive oil, and all the spices, salt, and pepper. Leave the chicken to marinate for at least 30 minutes (or up to 2 hours in the fridge).

Rinse the sliced potatoes under cold water to remove excess starch and pat dry. Layer them in a large baking tray and season lightly with salt and pepper.

In a separate bowl, mix the remaining garlic, lemon juice, and olive oil with the chopped coriander and water to make a fragrant dressing.

Place the marinated chicken pieces on top of the potatoes, skin side up. Pour the dressing all over the traybake, making sure the potatoes are well coated. Use your hands to rub everything in gently.

Cover the tray with foil and bake in a preheated oven at 200°C fan for 45 minutes. Uncover, baste the chicken in all the juices, then roast for another 25–30 minutes until golden and slightly crisp on top.

Serve hot in the tray alongside Lebanese rice with vermicelli or simple Lebanese salad, and lemon wedges.

Notes...

You can use chicken thighs or drumsticks if you prefer – whichever cut you choose, remember that bone-in chicken will always have better flavour.

For even more garlicky punch, leave some of the garlic cloves whole in the traybake and mash the roasted garlic into the potatoes before serving.

Don't skip the coriander – it gives the dish its southern character.

Leftovers (if there are any!) are even better the next day.

Samke Harra
سمكة حرّة

Spiced baked fish with tarator, pine nuts
& coriander

Serves 4–5

For the fish

1 whole sea bass or sea bream (1.2–
1.5kg), scaled and cleaned

60–80ml olive oil

2 tsp ground cumin

1½ tsp smoked paprika

½ tsp Aleppo chilli flakes, or to taste

½ tsp freshly ground black pepper

1½ tsp fine sea salt, or to taste

Juice of 3–4 large lemons

For the tarator

See page 202

5 tbsp olive oil

3 garlic cloves, finely grated

1 bunch fresh coriander, finely chopped
(about 80g)

1 green chilli, finely chopped (optional)

To finish

4 tbsp toasted pine nuts or walnuts

Pomegranate seeds (optional)

In Tripoli, the northern jewel of Lebanon, samke harra is more than just a seafood dish, it's pride on a plate. Walk through the old souks near the port and the scent of grilled fish and warm tahini fills the air. For us, Tripoli's most iconic dish was a celebratory meal for Eid, Sunday lunch, or when cousins came to visit from Beirut. It was a showstopper at every gathering, laid on a big tray, swimming in its nutty, lemony sauce, decorated with coriander and toasted nuts. Although it's called harra – meaning spicy – it's all about the balance of rich tahini, chilli heat, bright lemon, and fresh herbs.

Rinse the fish under cold water and pat dry with kitchen paper. Score the skin on both sides. Season inside and out with the olive oil, cumin, smoked paprika, chilli flakes, black pepper, salt, and lemon juice. Let it marinate for 20–30 minutes. Roast in a hot oven at 200°C fan for 25–30 minutes until the fish is cooked through and golden.

Meanwhile, make the tarator according to the recipe on page 202.

In a small pan, gently heat the olive oil. Sauté the finely grated garlic, coriander, and green chilli (if using) for 2–3 minutes until fragrant. Stir this mixture into the tarator and warm gently over low heat.

Place the cooked fish on a large serving platter. Spoon the warm tahini sauce generously over the fish, scatter with the toasted nuts and pomegranate seeds if using, then serve immediately.

Fasoulia b'Lahmé
فاصوليا باللحمة

A hearty pot of butter beans & lamb,
slowly simmered for deep flavour
Serves 4–5

60–80ml olive oil

600g bone-in lamb shoulder, cut into
150–200g chunks

1 large brown onion (about 200g), finely
chopped

8 large garlic cloves, finely grated

3 tbsp tomato paste

5 large ripe tomatoes (about 750g),
peeled and finely chopped or grated

1 large bunch fresh coriander (abut 80g),
washed and finely chopped (optional)

1½ tbsp fine sea salt, or to taste

½ tsp freshly ground black pepper

1 tbsp Baharat (Lebanese 7 spices)

2 bay leaves

1.5–2L cold water

2 large jars of good quality butter beans
(about 800–900g drained weight)

Fasoulia b'lahmé is true comfort food, a dish that reminds every Lebanese of home. When the smell of meat and garlic cooking together fills the kitchen, you know it's lunchtime. In our house, my mother would make it with fresh fasoulia in summer, and jarred butter beans throughout the rest of the year. The beans soak up the tomato broth and the flavour of the slow-cooked meat. With rice, lemon wedges, radishes, and crisp salad on the side, this dish needs nothing else – it brings the family straight to the table.

Heat the olive oil in a large pot over medium heat. Add the lamb and brown well on all sides. Add the finely chopped onion and sauté until soft and golden, then add the garlic and sauté gently for a minute until fragrant.

Add the tomato paste and stir well for 2 minutes, coating the meat and onions. Now add the fresh tomatoes. Cook gently for about 5–7 minutes, until the tomatoes have softened and the sauce begins to come together.

If using, add the chopped coriander directly into the pot. Stir to combine it with the tomato mixture and cook gently for a minute or two, allowing the coriander to release its aroma into the sauce.

Add the salt, black pepper, Baharat, and bay leaves, then pour in the water. Stir and bring to a gentle boil, skimming off any foam if needed.

Lower the heat and simmer gently, covered, for about 1.5–2 hours, stirring occasionally. The meat should be tender and the broth rich and well-flavoured.

Meanwhile, drain the butter beans and rinse gently under cold water. About 20 minutes before the end of the cooking time for the stew, add the butter beans to the pot. Stir gently and allow them to simmer in the broth, absorbing the flavours. The sauce should thicken slightly but remain loose enough to coat the rice beautifully. Taste and adjust the seasoning as needed before serving.

Serve hot alongside Lebanese rice with vermicelli, fresh radishes, pickles, and lemon wedges. A generous squeeze of lemon over the fasoulia brings everything to life – this is the way we eat it in our house.

Notes...

Try to buy fresh green butter beans in August
and September when they are in season,
available from good Middle Eastern stores
like Green Valley and Goodies in London.

Kafta b'Sayniyeh
كفتة بالصينية.

Kafta, potato & tomato traybake
Serves 4–5

For the kafta
See the recipe for Kafta Meshwiyé on page 149

For the sauce
5 large ripe tomatoes (about 750g), peeled and finely chopped or grated

3 tbsp tomato paste

4 tbsp olive oil

200ml water

Juice of 1 lemon

1 tbsp fine sea salt, or to taste

1 tsp freshly ground black pepper

1 tbsp Baharat (Lebanese 7 spices)

To assemble
4–5 medium Maris Piper potatoes (about 800g), peeled and sliced into 0.5cm thick rounds

Rapeseed oil, for shallow frying

Pinch of fine sea salt

2 large brown onions (about 400g), sliced into rounds

2 large ripe tomatoes, sliced into rounds

Notes...
This variation – with patties baked first and potatoes shallow fried – is popular in both North and South Lebanon.

Shallow frying the potatoes gives them a much better texture in the assembled dish, as they won't turn mushy in the sauce.

Forming kafta into patties makes serving the dish easier – a beautiful meal for family gatherings.

Kafta b'sayniyeh is loved across all of Lebanon – you'll find it on family tables from Zgharta to Jezzine, from the old quarters of Saida to the kitchens of Baalbek and the Békaa villages. Some make it as one layered dish, others, like in the North, form kafta into patties, bake them, and then build the dish with crispy potatoes and rich tomato sauce. In the South, many households shallow-fry the potatoes first so the edges stay golden and full of flavour. However it's done, kafta b'sayniyeh is one of the country's great comfort dishes, best served with rice, bread, and family.

To prepare and cook the kafta
Preheat your oven to 200°C (180°C fan). For this recipe, when you have made your kafta mixture according to the recipe on page 149, shape it into round patties about 6–7cm wide and 1cm thick (you should have 8–10 patties).

Place the patties on a baking tray lined with baking paper. Bake in the oven for 12–15 minutes, until lightly browned but not fully cooked through as they will finish cooking in the sauce. Leave the oven on ready to bake the assembled dish.

To prepare the sauce
In a bowl, mix the all the ingredients together until thoroughly combined.

To assemble the traybake
Heat a shallow layer of oil in a large frying pan. Lightly season the potato slices with salt. Shallow fry the potato in batches until golden on both sides but not too crispy – the slices should stay tender. Drain on kitchen paper.

Scatter half of the sliced onions into a large baking dish or tray (about 30 x 25cm). Arrange the fried potato slices and baked kafta patties in layers over the onion – you can alternate them or lay them side by side. Scatter the remaining onions and sliced tomatoes over the top. Pour the sauce evenly over everything (it should come about three quarters up the sides of the dish – add a little more water if needed).

Cover with foil and bake in the hot oven for 30–35 minutes. Remove the foil and bake uncovered for another 20–25 minutes, until the sauce is thickened and bubbling, and the top is slightly caramelised. Let it rest for 5–10 minutes before serving.

Serve hot alongside Lebanese rice with vermicelli, warm khobez, and lemon wedges. In our house, the fight was always for the best browned potatoes on top!

Maghmour
مغمور بالفرن

Lebanon's moussaka: aubergine baked
with chickpeas, tomato & olive oil
Serves 4–5

3 medium aubergines (about 900g), cut
into 4–5cm cubes

60–80ml extra virgin olive oil, plus extra
for frying

2 medium brown onions, finely sliced

6 garlic cloves, finely grated

2 tbsp tomato paste

500g ripe tomatoes, peeled and
chopped, or 400g best quality tinned
chopped tomatoes

1 tbsp dried mint, plus extra for sprinkling

1 tsp ground cumin

1½ tsp fine sea salt, or to taste

1 tsp freshly ground black pepper

400ml water or light vegetable stock

200g dried chickpeas, soaked overnight,
or 1 x 400g jar of cooked chickpeas

2 medium tomatoes, sliced (for layering
on top)

To serve

Warm khobez

Chilli pickles

Lemon wedges

Notes...

Maghmour is all about clean flavours, proper
olive oil, gentle heat, and patience. Like my
mother always said: 'Don't rush maghmour.
Let it sit, let it melt together.'

The cumin and dried mint bring the whole
dish to life.

Maghmour takes me straight back to the small southern
villages where neighbours shared what they grew.
Aubergines from the garden, chickpeas from last season,
tomatoes ripened under the sun. The women salted
the aubergines early, frying them while chatting in the
courtyard. By afternoon, every house smelled of garlic,
mint, and cumin as the trays baked slowly, ready to join a
simple table of khobez, lemons, and good company.

To prepare the aubergines

Lightly salt the aubergine cubes and place in a colander for 30
minutes to release any bitterness and excess water. Rinse and pat
completely dry with kitchen paper.

Heat some olive oil in a wide pan and shallow fry the aubergines in
batches until golden. Drain on kitchen paper and set aside.

To prepare the tomato sauce

In a wide saucepan, heat the extra virgin olive oil over medium heat.
Add the onions and sauté for 8–10 minutes until soft and translucent.
Stir in the garlic and cook for another minute. Now add the tomato
paste and stir for 1–2 minutes to release its aroma, then add the
chopped tomatoes, dried mint, cumin, fine sea salt, and black pepper.

Stir the tomato mixture well and then pour in the water or stock.
Bring to a simmer. If you are using dried and soaked chickpeas, drain
them and add to the sauce at this stage. Simmer gently for 35–40
minutes until tender. Taste and adjust the seasoning.

If you are using jarred chickpeas, let the sauce simmer for 15 minutes,
then add the chickpeas and cook for an additional 15–20 minutes to
allow the flavours to absorb.

To assemble and bake

Preheat your oven to 180°C (160°C fan). Take a large baking tray
(about 30 x 22cm) and layer the fried aubergine evenly across the
base. Pour the rich tomato and chickpea sauce evenly on top. Arrange
the sliced tomatoes over the surface, then drizzle with a little extra
virgin olive oil and sprinkle with dried mint.

Cover the tray loosely with foil and bake in the oven for 30 minutes.
Remove the foil and bake uncovered for 15–20 minutes until the top
slightly caramelises and the sauce thickens beautifully.

Let it rest at room temperature for 15 minutes, then serve warm or at
room temperature with fresh khobez, pickles, and lemon wedges.

Bazella b'Lahmé
بازيلا باللحمة

Lebanese-style lamb, peas & carrots in
hearty tomato sauce
Serves 4–5

60–80ml olive oil

600g lamb shoulder or beef shin, cut into
large cubes

1 medium brown onion (about 200g),
finely chopped

8 garlic cloves, finely grated

3 tbsp tomato paste

5 large ripe tomatoes (about 750g),
peeled and finely chopped or grated

1 large bunch fresh coriander, washed
and finely chopped

1 tbsp fine sea salt, or to taste

½ tsp freshly ground black pepper

1 tbsp Baharat (Lebanese 7 spices)

1.5–2L water

4 large carrots (about 300g), peeled and
diced or sliced into thin rounds

600g frozen peas (or 800g shelled fresh
peas when in season)

Bazella b'lahmé is one of the most loved and familiar tabkha across all of Lebanon. It is a true family dish, often the first stew children learn to eat. In the South, in Beirut, in the mountains, every home makes its own version, but the essentials remain the same: tender lamb or beef, a rich tomato broth, sweet peas, and soft carrots. Some families like a lighter broth, others a thicker one to spoon over rice. In our house, my mother always added plenty of coriander which gave the dish a bright, unmistakable flavour. In season, she used fresh peas from the market but for everyday cooking, good-quality frozen peas make it an easy and delicious dish all year round.

Heat the olive oil in a large pot over medium heat. Add the lamb or beef and brown well on all sides. Add the finely chopped onion and sauté until soft and golden, then add the garlic and sauté gently for a minute until fragrant.

Add the tomato paste and stir well for 2 minutes, coating the meat and onions. Now add the fresh tomatoes. Cook gently for about 5–7 minutes, until the tomatoes have softened and the sauce begins to come together.

Add the chopped coriander directly into the pot. Stir to combine it with the tomato mixture and cook gently for a minute or two, allowing the coriander to release its aroma into the sauce.

Add the salt, black pepper, and Baharat, then pour in the water. Stir and bring to a gentle boil, skimming off any foam if needed.

Lower the heat and simmer gently, covered, for about 1.5–2 hours, stirring occasionally. The meat should be tender and the broth rich and well-flavoured.

Add the diced carrots to the pot and simmer for about 15 minutes. Then add the peas and simmer for a further 15–20 minutes, until both the carrots and peas are tender and have absorbed the flavour of the sauce.

Taste and adjust the seasoning as needed. The sauce should be balanced, rich with tomato and coriander, and just loose enough to coat the rice beautifully. Serve hot alongside Lebanese rice, warm khobez, radishes, pickles, and lemon wedges.

Rez m'Falfal
رز بالشعيرية

Lebanese rice with vermicelli
Serves 4–5

2 tbsp olive oil, 2 tbsp samneh or a mix of both (this is authentic and gives best flavour)

100g fine wheat vermicelli

300g basmati or long-grain rice, washed and soaked in cold water for 20 minutes, then drained

600ml boiling water, or light chicken broth if you want extra flavour

2 tsp fine sea salt, or to taste

In every Lebanese home, rice with vermicelli is the standard companion to tabkha. It may be simple, but it must be done with care. The rice must be light and fluffy, and the vermicelli golden, never greasy or heavy. In our house, my mother cooked this almost daily. The sound of the vermicelli toasting in olive oil or samneh was the first sign that lunch was coming. It is not just a side dish though – it soaks up the broth of the tabkha, balances strong flavours, and completes the table.

Heat the olive oil, samneh or both in a heavy-bottomed pot over medium heat. Add the vermicelli and sauté gently, stirring constantly, until it turns a rich golden brown. Watch it carefully so the vermicelli does not burn.

Once the vermicelli is evenly golden, add the drained rice. Stir gently to coat the rice with the oil and vermicelli. Add the boiling water and salt. Stir once to combine, then bring back to a gentle boil.

Turn the heat down as low as possible, cover the pot tightly with a lid, and let it simmer undisturbed for 25–28 minutes. Do not lift the lid or move the pot during cooking.

When the rice is ready, it should be tender, the grains separate and fluffy. Remove from the heat and let it rest, covered, for 5 minutes.

Fluff gently with a fork before serving. Serve hot with your tabkha, mloukhieh, fasoulia, and bemieh – this is the true Lebanese way.

Notes...

Using samneh and olive oil together gives the best flavour.

Always toast the vermicelli carefully – it gives the rice its signature aroma.

Basmati rice is commonly used today, but in the old days we used local long-grain rice. Both are excellent.

Réz b'Dfine
رز بدفين

Fragrant rice with tender oxtail, cooked
in rich broth
Serves 4–5

For the broth
1.5kg fresh oxtail, cut into 100–150g
chunks

60–80ml olive oil

4L cold water

1 large brown onion, peeled and
quartered

2 bay leaves

1 cinnamon stick

6 black peppercorns

1 tsp fine sea salt, or to taste

For the rice
2 tbsp olive oil

2 tbsp samneh (or clarified butter)

3 medium brown onions, thinly sliced

4 large garlic cloves, finely grated

350g long grain or basmati rice, rinsed

1½ tsp Baharat (Lebanese 7 spices)

½ tsp ground cinnamon

1 tsp freshly ground black pepper, to
taste

1½ tsp fine sea salt, or to taste

200g jarred chickpeas, rinsed and
drained

Réz b'dfine is not a dish you find in restaurants – it's home
food. It's the kind of dish that fills the house with its rich
aroma for hours before lunch is served. I still remember
my father bringing home the oxtail, carefully selected and
wrapped in butchers' paper, while my mother soaked the
chickpeas overnight in a large ceramic bowl. Early the next
morning, she would clean the oxtail with salt and lemon
– as every Lebanese mother does – and begin simmering
the broth. The scent of bay leaves, Baharat, cinnamon,
and black pepper would slowly rise from the pot, travelling
up the building's stairwell. By lunchtime, the oxtail was
melting off the bone, the chickpeas buttery soft, and the
rice full of flavour, all gently resting in the deeply spiced
broth. We would gather around the table, bowls filled, with
fresh lemon wedges, raw onions, and khobez on the side.

To prepare the broth
First, clean the oxtail thoroughly. Rinse under cold water, rub with
salt and lemon juice, rinse again, and pat dry.

Heat the oil in a large pan over medium heat. Add the oxtail and
brown well on all sides, then cover with the cold water and bring
to a boil. Skim off any foam and when the water is clear, add the
remaining ingredients for the broth. Lower the heat, cover the pan
and simmer for 2–2.5 hours until the meat is tender. Check every 30
minutes. When ready, strain the broth and then set both the broth
and the cooked oxtail aside.

To cook the rice
In a wide pot, heat the oil with the samneh. Add the sliced onion and
cook until golden and soft, then add the grated garlic and cook for a
few minutes. Add the rinsed rice and stir gently to coat each grain.
Add the spices and salt, then stir for 1–2 minutes until the spices
release their aroma. Add the drained chickpeas to the rice and pour in
enough hot broth to cover the rice by about 1.5cm (about 600–700ml,
depending on your pot). Stir once and taste to check the seasoning.

Gently place the oxtail pieces on top of the rice. Bring to a boil, cover,
reduce the heat to low, and simmer for 24–26 minutes until the rice is
cooked and the broth has been absorbed.

Once the rice is ready, serve with plenty of lemon wedges and
warm khobez. The true Lebanese way is simple – let everyone help
themselves and enjoy at the table together.

Mloukhieh
ملوخية بالدجاج

Earthy jute mallow with tender chicken
in a fragrant broth
Serves 4–5

For the broth
1–1.2kg whole chicken

2–2.5L cold water

1 large brown onion (about 200g), halved

2–3 bay leaves

1 cinnamon stick

4 cardamom pods

2 cloves

For the stew
100g dried mloukhieh leaves

3 medium brown onions (about 300g),
peeled and quartered

12 large garlic cloves, peeled

60–80ml olive oil

1 large bunch fresh coriander (about
80g), leaves washed, picked and chopped

1½ tbsp ground coriander

1½ tbsp fine sea salt, or to taste

½ tsp freshly ground black pepper

Juice of 2 large lemons

To serve
Lebanese rice with vermicelli (see page
126)

1 white onion, finely diced and pickled in
grape vinegar for 10–15 minutes

Lemon wedges

Warm khobez

Notes...
Roasting the onion and garlic deepens the flavour
beautifully – this small step makes a big difference
to the dish.

Always use plenty of coriander, which gives
mloukhieh its true Lebanese soul.

Dry mloukhieh should be soaked and drained
properly to preserve its delicate texture.

Always serve this dish with plenty of lemon wedges
– the balance of flavours depends on it.

For many Lebanese families, dried mloukhieh (mallow
leaf) is the most traditional way to prepare this dish. In
the villages, fresh leaves were hung and dried in summer,
then stored in cloth bags to cook with all year. My mother
always preferred the dried leaves because they have a deeper
flavour and the texture is lighter, almost silky. I remember
her soaking them in the morning, the kitchen filling
with the smell of coriander and garlic as the mloukhieh
simmered later in the day. The table would be set with rice,
onion, lemons, and bread – nothing fancy, just good home
cooked food.

Place the chicken in a large bowl and rinse thoroughly under cold
water. Transfer to a large pot, cover with 2 litres of cold water, and
bring to a boil over medium heat. As soon as the broth comes to a
boil, skim off any scum or foam that rises to the surface.

Once the broth is clear, add the onion, bay leaves, cinnamon stick,
cardamom pods, and cloves. Lower the heat and simmer gently for
about 50–60 minutes, or until the chicken is tender and cooked
through. Remove the chicken and set aside. Strain the broth through
a fine sieve and return it to the pot. Discard the aromatics left in the
sieve.

While the chicken is cooking, soak the dried mloukhieh leaves in cold
water for 45–60 minutes, changing the water once or twice. Drain
well and gently squeeze out the excess water. Spread the leaves on a
clean kitchen towel to dry slightly.

Preheat the oven to 180°C (160°C fan). Place the quartered onions
and whole garlic cloves on a small baking tray, then drizzle with olive
oil and season with salt and ground coriander. Roast for about 25–30
minutes, until soft and golden. Transfer to a food processor and blitz
to a coarse paste.

Heat the olive oil in a large frying pan over medium heat. Add the
roasted onion and garlic paste and sauté gently for 2–3 minutes
until fragrant. Add the finely chopped coriander and cook for
another 2 minutes until the mixture is aromatic and softened. Add
the drained mloukhieh leaves to the pan and sauté for 3–4 minutes,
stirring gently.

Transfer the sautéed mloukhieh mixture to the clear chicken broth.
Simmer gently for 20–25 minutes, stirring occasionally. Meanwhile,
shred the cooked chicken by hand into large pieces and add them
back to the pot. Simmer for another 5–10 minutes to bring the
flavours together. Season with ground coriander, salt, black pepper,
and lemon juice. Taste and adjust as needed – mloukhieh should have
a bright, lemony finish.

Serve hot with Lebanese rice, pickled diced onion, lemon wedges, and
warm khobez.

Sélée Mehshi
سلق محشي

Stuffed chard leaves with rice, mince &
lemony broth
Serves 4–5

For the stuffed chard

2 large bunches Swiss chard (about 1kg),
ideally with large leaves

2L water, for blanching

1½ tbsp fine sea salt, or to taste

400g lamb shoulder or beef and lamb
mix, freshly minced

2 large brown onions (about 400g), finely
chopped

250g short grain rice, washed and
drained

5–6 large garlic cloves, finely grated

100ml olive oil

1 tbsp tomato paste

1½ tbsp Baharat (Lebanese 7 spices)

1 tsp freshly ground black pepper

For the base and broth

2 large potatoes (about 400g)

2 large brown onions

2 large tomatoes (about 300g)

8–10 large garlic cloves, finely grated

Juice of 5–6 large lemons

4–6 tbsp olive oil

500ml water

1 tbsp fine sea salt, or to taste

1½ tsp Baharat

For the tahini dip

300–400g reserved chard stalks

2–3 garlic cloves, finely grated

150g tahini

Juice of 1 lemon

4–6 tbsp cold water

Pinch of fine sea salt

For me, sélée mehshi is one of those dishes that brings back
fading early memories. I remember coming home from
school in Beirut and opening the door to the warm scent
of garlic, lemon and simmering chard filling the house.
In those moments, the old kitchen, the wooden table, the
steam on the windows all felt like pure comfort. At home,
mothers prepare this dish with love – rolling each leaf
by hand, lining the pot with potatoes and tomatoes, and
serving it with a creamy dip made from the chard stalks.
'Nothing from sélée goes in the bin,' my mother would
always say. This is true village cooking – economical,
generous, full of flavour. Even today, the first bite takes me
straight back to that cosy kitchen of my childhood.

To prepare the stuffed chard

Wash the Swiss chard well. Cut off the thick stalks and reserve them
for the tahini dip. Bring the water to a boil with 1 tablespoon of the
salt. Blanch the chard leaves in batches for 10–15 seconds, just until
flexible. Drain under cold water then pat dry gently with clean towel.

In a large bowl, combine all the remaining ingredients to make the
filling. Place a chard leaf on a flat surface, shiny side down. Add 1
tablespoon of filling near the base. Fold the sides in and roll up tightly
but not too firmly. Repeat with all the leaves and filling.

To prepare the base and broth

Peel the potatoes and onions, then slice these and the tomatoes into
0.5cm rounds. Line the base of a wide pot with the potato slices,
then layer the onion and tomato slices on top. This prevents sticking
and adds flavour to the broth. Pack the prepared chard rolls tightly in
layers over the base.

In a large jug, combine the garlic, lemon juice, olive oil, water, salt,
and Baharat. Pour this broth over the rolls – it should nearly cover
them. Place a small heatproof plate on top to keep the rolls in place.
Bring to a gentle boil, then cover, lower the heat, and simmer for
50–60 minutes until the leaves and rice are cooked and tender. Rest
for 10–15 minutes before serving, while you make the dip.

To prepare the tahini dip

Blanch the reserved chard stalks in salted water until tender, about
5–7 minutes. Drain well. Blend the stalks with the garlic, tahini,
lemon juice, and enough cold water to make a smooth, creamy dip.
Season with salt to taste.

Arrange the rolls on a platter, spooning some of the broth over them.
Serve the potato, onion and tomato base from the pot as part of the
dish. Serve the tahini dip on the side for dipping the rolls or eating
with khobez. Always serve with extra lemon wedges.

Sheikh el Mehshi
شيخ المحشي

Baked baby aubergines stuffed with
spiced mince in rich tomato sauce
Serves 4–5

For the aubergines
12–16 firm, small, evenly-sized
aubergines (about 1–1.2kg)
1L rapeseed oil, for shallow frying

For the filling
50ml olive oil

2 large brown onions, finely chopped

4 garlic cloves, finely grated

500g lamb shoulder or lamb and beef
mix, freshly minced

1 tbsp Baharat (Lebanese 7 spices)

½ tsp freshly ground black pepper

2 tsp fine sea salt, or to taste

4 tbsp pine nuts, toasted

For the sauce
6 large ripe tomatoes (about 900g),
peeled and finely chopped or grated

3 tbsp tomato paste

4–5 tbsp olive oil

200ml water

Juice of 1 lemon

2 tsp fine sea salt, or to taste

½ tsp freshly ground black pepper

2 tsp Baharat

To assemble
2 large tomatoes, sliced

1 tbsp dried mint

Notes...
Use enough oil to cover at least half the
aubergines when shallow frying.

Sheikh el mehshi is one of those dishes that you will find on
the table in homes from Akkar to Jezzine, from the villages
of Keserwan to the old houses of Tripoli and Saida. The
aubergines are hollowed only lightly, leaving enough flesh
to hold their shape and soak up the sauce beautifully. And
they are always shallow-fried first, until golden and tender.
My mother said that 'if you skip the frying, it's not sheikh el
mehshi – it's just stuffed aubergines.' Every family has their
touch – more lemon in the South, more pine nuts in the
North – but one thing is always the same, that this is a dish
of patience, celebration, and love.

To prepare the aubergines
Wash the aubergines well. Cut off the stems neatly. Using a corer,
carefully create a small hollow inside each aubergine, leaving about
0.5–0.7cm of flesh between the core and the skin so they hold their
shape and stay juicy inside.

In a deep, wide frying pan, heat the oil on medium heat. Shallow
fry the aubergines in batches, turning them gently with tongs, until
golden on all sides and just tender. This should take 4–5 minutes per
side. Drain on kitchen paper.

To prepare the filling
Heat the olive oil in a large pan. Sauté the onions until golden, then
stir in the garlic. Add the minced meat and cook, breaking it up, until
browned. Season with the Baharat, black pepper, and salt. Stir in the
toasted pine nuts, then leave the filling to cool slightly before stuffing
the aubergines generously, leaving a small gap at the top.

To prepare the sauce
Mix the tomatoes, tomato paste, olive oil, water, lemon juice, salt,
black pepper, and Baharat together in a jug or bowl.

To assemble the dish
Arrange the stuffed aubergines tightly in a wide pot or deep baking
dish, keeping them in a single layer if possible. Pour the sauce over
and around them – it should almost cover the aubergines. If needed,
add a little more water to top it up. Place a slice of tomato on top of
each aubergine and sprinkle with the dried mint.

Cover the pot or dish with a lid or foil. Cook gently on the stovetop for
about 50–60 minutes on low heat or bake at 180°C for about 1 hour,
until the aubergines are tender but still holding their shape, and the
sauce is thick and rich.

Let it rest for 10 minutes before serving alongside Lebanese rice with
vermicelli. The sauce spooned over the rice is always the best part.

Burghul w Djej
برغل و دجاج

Nutty burghul cooked in broth with
tender chicken

Serves 4–5

For the chicken and broth

1 whole free-range chicken (1.2–1.5kg)

1.5–2L cold water

1 onion, peeled and halved

1 small cinnamon stick

2–3 cardamom pods

1 bay leaf

2 whole cloves

5 black peppercorns

1 tbsp fine sea salt, or to taste

3 tbsp olive oil

¼ tsp freshly ground black pepper

¼ tsp Baharat (Lebanese 7 spices)

For the burghul

3 tbsp olive oil

1 tbsp samneh or vegetable oil

200g brown onion, finely chopped

4 garlic cloves, finely grated

350g coarse brown burghul wheat,
washed with cold water and drained

1 tbsp Baharat

½ tsp ground cumin

2 tsp fine sea salt, or to taste

½ tsp freshly ground black pepper

200g cooked chickpeas (or 1 x 400g jar
of chickpeas, drained and rinsed)

700–800ml hot chicken stock

2 tbsp pine nuts, toasted

2 tbsp slivered almonds, toasted

There's something timeless about this dish, found from the
wheat fields of the Békaa to the quiet courtyards of Akkar.
You don't need much to make it sing – good olive oil, sweet
onions, nutty bulgur and chicken that's been browned
just enough to give depth. Chickpeas stretch the dish,
cinnamon and clove lift it, and the result is one of those
'tray on the floor, sit cross-legged' kind of meals – simple,
rustic, but full of soul.

To prepare the chicken and broth

Rinse the chicken thoroughly in a large pot, then cover with the cold
water and bring to a boil. Skim off any foam and when the water is
clear, add the onion, whole spices, and salt. Reduce the heat and
simmer for 50–60 minutes until the chicken is fully cooked.

Remove the chicken from the pot and set aside. Strain the broth,
discarding the solids left in the sieve, and keep it hot. Once cool
enough to handle, portion the chicken into large pieces. In a wide pan,
heat the olive oil. Season the chicken with the remaining spices. Sear
each piece on both sides over medium heat until lightly golden, then
cover and set aside.

To prepare the burghul

Heat the olive oil and samneh in a pot. Add the chopped onion and
garlic, then sauté for 10–12 minutes until soft and golden. Add the
burghul and stir for 2–3 minutes to toast the grains. Add the spices,
salt, and pepper. Mix well, taste and adjust the seasoning if needed,
then stir in the chickpeas.

Pour in just enough of the reserved hot chicken stock to cover the
burghul by about 1.5–1.8cm. Bring to a gentle boil, then lower the
heat, cover, and simmer for 20–25 minutes until the burghul is tender
and all the stock has been absorbed. Turn off the heat and let it rest,
covered, for 10 minutes.

Fluff the burghul gently. Spoon onto a wide serving dish and arrange
the seared chicken pieces over the top. Garnish with the toasted pine
nuts and almonds. Serve warm, with laban b'khyar and khobez on
the side.

Notes...

This dish depends on each step being done with care – the broth must be
aromatic and clean, the burghul cooked gently, and the final touch of searing
brings the dish back to life. No shortcuts, no nonsense, just a good plate of
food the way our mothers made it.

If you like, you can serve this with a salatet banadoura (see page 63) instead
of laban b'khyar.

Moghrabieh
مغربية

Semolina pearls, spiced chicken &
onions in caraway-scented sauce
Serves 4–5

For the broth

1 whole chicken (about 1.5kg), cut into 6
pieces

4L water

2 large brown onions (about 400g),
halved

2 bay leaves

1 cinnamon stick

3 cardamom pods

1 tsp whole black peppercorns

1 tsp fine sea salt

For the moghrabieh

3 tbsp olive oil

3 tbsp butter or samneh

500g dry moghrabieh

200g jarred or freshly cooked chickpeas
(see page 80)

2 tsp Baharat (Lebanese 7 spices)

2 tsp caraway powder

1 tbsp fine sea salt, or to taste

½ tsp freshly ground black pepper

In Beirut, moghrabieh is an occasion dish – not something you cook every day, but a meal to prepare for family gatherings. I remember my mother making it in the old apartment – the scent of caraway and cumin would fill the building, and neighbours would knock just to ask, 'is it moghrabieh today?'. The dish is known across Lebanon, from the streets of Beirut to the homes of Saida, Tripoli, and Zahlé with each region adding its own touch. In Beirut, it is often made with chicken, richly spiced, and served in broth with soft onions and buttery pearl couscous. It is a dish that feeds the body and the soul – pure comfort food from home.

Rinse the chicken thoroughly in a large pot, then cover with the cold water and bring to a boil. Skim off any foam that forms on the surface and when the water is clear, add all other ingredients for the broth. Reduce the heat and simmer for 50–60 minutes until the chicken is fully cooked. Remove the chicken pieces and set aside. Strain the broth through a fine sieve and reserve, keeping it hot. Discard the aromatics left in the sieve.

Heat the olive oil and butter or samneh for the mograbieh in a large pot. Add the moghrabieh pearls and toast gently while stirring for 5–7 minutes, until lightly golden and fragrant, then add the chickpeas and stir well. Pour over about 1.5–2 litres of the reserved hot broth, to cover the pearls. Season with the Baharat, caraway, salt, and black pepper. Simmer gently, stirring occasionally and adding more broth as needed, for 20–25 minutes until the pearls are tender but not mushy. Set aside and keep warm.

In a large pan, heat the olive oil and butter or samneh for the onions and chickpeas. Add the baby onions and sauté gently until golden and just tender, about 10–12 minutes. Add the chickpeas and season with the caraway, cinnamon, salt, and pepper. Add 300ml of the reserved hot broth, cover, and simmer gently for 10–15 minutes until the onions are soft and fragrant.

For the baby onions & chickpeas

2 tbsp olive oil

2 tbsp butter or samneh

300g baby round onions, peeled

200g jarred or freshly cooked chickpeas

1½ tsp caraway powder

1 tsp ground cinnamon

Fine sea salt and black pepper, to taste

For the chicken

2 tbsp olive oil or samneh

1½ tsp Baharat

½ tsp ground cinnamon

Pinch of fine sea salt, to taste

For the gravy

3 tbsp olive oil

3 tbsp butter or samneh

3 tbsp plain flour

600ml reserved hot chicken broth

While the other components are cooking, rub the chicken pieces with the olive oil or samneh, Baharat, cinnamon, and a little salt. Place on a tray and roast in the oven at 200°C (180°C fan) for 10–15 minutes until golden. Set aside and keep warm.

In a separate pan, heat the olive oil and butter or samneh for the gravy. Stir in the flour and cook gently while whisking for 2–3 minutes until pale golden. Gradually whisk in the hot broth to form a smooth, velvety gravy. Simmer gently until slightly thickened, just enough to coat the back of a spoon.

Stir the cooked baby onions and chickpeas into the gravy. Taste and adjust the seasoning – the sauce should be rich, warmly spiced, and well balanced.

Spoon the moghrabieh pearls into a large serving platter. Arrange the golden, spiced chicken pieces on top or alongside, then spoon the baby onion and chickpea gravy generously over the top.

Notes...

Finishing the chicken with Baharat and a golden colour from roasting is essential – this is how mothers in Beirut prepare it.

The baby onions in the gravy should be golden and soft, never raw or crunchy.

The gravy must be silky and not too thick.

Caraway and cinnamon are the signature spices in this dish, so use them boldly.

Mashawi

Barbecue, the Lebanese way

In Lebanon, barbecuing isn't just a method of cooking, it's a way of life.
Come Sunday, you'll find grills smoking in every corner of the country –
on balconies in Beirut, on rooftops in Tripoli, in gardens tucked between
olive trees, or under the shade of pine forests in the mountains. If there's
space to set up a mangal and light some coal, it's enough. The Lebanese
will make it work. We don't need fancy gear, just good meat, friends or
family, and the excuse to gather.

It's always more than just lunch. Mashawi can become the whole day, from
prepping to grilling, snacking, joking, maybe arguing over who does the
fire better. And if you're heading out on a proper day trip, it becomes
a production. That's what I remember most from my childhood. When
we didn't barbecue at home, we'd pack up the car early and head towards
the river. Not one of those touristy places – we'd drive until we found the
quiet spots, tucked between rocks and trees, where the sound of the water
was loud and the air smelled of thyme and smoke.

Everyone had a role. My sisters would be mixing the tabbouleh, someone
would be skewering the meat, while my mum made sure nothing was
forgotten (especially the arghileh). My dad and brothers-in-law lit the
coals like they were starting a campfire in the wild, fiercely protective
of their technique. And someone would find a deep, cold pocket in the
stream to wedge the watermelon in between the rocks, letting the water
chill it until it was time to slice it open.

We'd start with olives, bread, and a bit of hummus for dipping, while the
smell of charcoal and marinated meat filled the air. Kafta, lahmé, taouk:
each one placed carefully on the grill, flipped and basted with a small
squeeze of fresh lemon juice or brushed with pomegranate molasses. No
cutlery, no plates, just khobez wrapped around the grilled meat with a
handful of pickles, charred baby onion, or onion salad.

And when the food was done and bellies were full, we didn't rush to leave.
That's when the coffee would go on – real Lebanese coffee, thick and
strong, cooked slowly in the embers of the dying fire. We'd sip it barefoot
on the rocks, the kids still swimming, the watermelon now cold and
perfect.

This is barbecue, the Lebanese way – food, family, nature, and a whole lot
of time to enjoy all three.

Jawaneh Meshwé
جوانح بالثوم

Chicken wings with garlic, coriander,
lemon & chilli

Serves 4–5

For the marinated wings

1.2kg chicken wings, cleaned and tips
trimmed

6–8 large garlic cloves, finely grated

1½ tbsp fine sea salt, or to taste

1 tbsp Baharat (Lebanese 7 spices)

½ tsp ground coriander

1 tsp smoked paprika

1 tsp freshly ground black pepper

Juice of 2 large lemons

2 tbsp apple cider vinegar

4 tbsp olive oil

For the sauce

Large handful of fresh coriander leaves,
very finely chopped (about 40g)

1 small red chilli, deseeded and finely
chopped (or leave seeds in for extra heat)

4–6 garlic cloves, finely grated

Zest and juice of 1 lemon

4 tbsp olive oil

Pinch of salt

If you grew up in Lebanon, you'll know the smell of charcoal-grilled jawaneh. It's the scent of rooftops in summer, of plastic tables pulled into alleyways, of cousins fighting over who gets the crispiest wing. In Tyre, it was the beach; in Beirut, it was the roof of our building; in the mountains, it was always under the pine trees. The marinade would already be soaking into the wings by noon, ready for a sunset grill with loud music, pickles, and half-cut lemons on the side. This wasn't a sit-down meal – it was standing, chatting, dipping, licking your fingers, and wiping your mouth with khobez.

To prepare and cook the wings

Pat the cleaned and trimmed wings fully dry. Combine all the remaining ingredients until thick and fragrant to make the marinade.

Pour the marinade over the wings, coat them thoroughly, then cover and marinate for at least 4 hours or overnight in the fridge.

Bring the marinated wings to room temperature before cooking. Grill over charcoal until golden, crisp, and lightly charred, flipping and basting often. Alternatively, you can oven-roast the wings at 220°C (200°C fan) for 35–40 minutes, then briefly finish them under a hot grill to char the skins.

To prepare the sauce and serve

Simply mix all the ingredients for the sauce together in a large bowl. Toss the grilled wings in the garlic-coriander-chilli sauce and serve straight away with lemon wedges, toum (see page 203), and fries.

Kastaleta
كستليتا

Lamb chops grilled over hot coals,
marinated in garlic, lemon & Baharat
Serves 4–5

1.2–1.5kg lamb chops or ribs (French-
trimmed if possible)

5 tbsp extra virgin olive oil

Juice of 1 large lemon

6 garlic cloves, finely grated

2 tbsp finely chopped fresh thyme

1½ tbsp pomegranate molasses

1 tbsp Baharat (Lebanese 7 spices)

1 tbsp sumac

1½ tsp fine sea salt

1 tsp freshly ground black pepper

Kastaleta was always reserved for those big meals that brought the family together at Eid, on Sundays, or when someone returned from travel. Marinating would start the day before, and the scent of garlic and spices would drift through the kitchen. My mother would press the chops into the mixture with her hands, making sure every piece was covered. On the day of the meal, my dad would light the charcoal, and when it was ready to serve you'd hear the sizzle before the platter even reached the table. In our neighbourhood, it was a dish that travelled over garden walls – everyone knew when it was kastaleta day. We'd eat them hot off the grill, with pickles, fattoush, and bread for tearing and sharing in the middle of the table.

Combine all the ingredients in a large bowl or tray and mix by hand until the chops are thoroughly coated. Cover and marinate in the fridge for at least 4 hours, ideally overnight.

Remove the marinated chops from the fridge and let them sit at room temperature for 30–45 minutes before grilling.

Grill over hot charcoal or in a cast iron pan for 3–4 minutes on each side until seared and just cooked through. Rest for 5 minutes before serving.

Serve with pickled turnips, fattoush or tabbouleh, and warm khobez.

Kafta Meshwiyé
كفتة مشوية

Charcoal-grilled minced meat skewers
with tarator & téblé salad
Serves 4–5

1 large bunch flat-leaf parsley

1 large brown onion (about 200g)

700g minced lamb shoulder, minced
beef, or a 50/50 mix with some fat

2 tsp Baharat (Lebanese 7 spices)

1½ tsp fine sea salt, or to taste

1 tsp ground nutmeg

½ tsp freshly ground black pepper

Kafta was one of those dependable dishes that's fast, filling, and always on hand for surprise guests. Whether grilled on skewers over charcoal, baked with potatoes in tomato sauce, or shaped into patties and seared in a pan, kafta was on rotation weekly. We would often make it on Fridays, eaten with fresh téblé salad, tarator, and always plenty of bread. I remember sitting on the steps, helping my mum pick parsley – a small task that somehow made me feel like I was part of something bigger.

Wash the parsley thoroughly, dry it completely, and chop the leaves finely – you should have about 80–100g. Peel and grate the onion, then squeeze out some of the liquid if it's too watery. In a large bowl, combine the minced meat, parsley, onion, salt, and spices. Mix by hand until well combined and slightly sticky.

Shape the mixture into oval patties, long fingers, or skewers. Grill over charcoal for 3–4 minutes on each side until nicely charred and cooked through. You can also sear the kafta in a hot pan or bake them in the oven.

Serve hot with téblé salad (see page 153), tarator (see page 202), warm khobez, and pickled cucumber.

Notes...

Always use fresh, flat-leaf (not curly) parsley and don't skip it. It's what gives kafta its Lebanese identity.

If grilling over charcoal, soak wooden skewers in water for 30 minutes before using them – but it's better to use metal skewers.

If preparing in advance, refrigerate the mixture for 1 hour before shaping as this helps the kafta hold together on the grill.

Leftover kafta can be wrapped in flatbread to enjoy the next day (see the sandwiché recipe on page 176).

Farrouj Meshwé
فروج مشوي

Charcoal-grilled spatchcock chicken
with toum & fries
Serves 4–5

1 free-range chicken, spatchcocked
(about 1.2–1.5kg)

Juice of 2 large lemons

6 tbsp olive oil

10 large garlic cloves, finely grated

3 tbsp pepper paste

2 tbsp apple cider vinegar

1 tbsp Baharat (Lebanese 7 spices)

1 tbsp fine sea salt, or to taste

1 tsp freshly ground black pepper

1 tbsp smoked paprika

I'd hold my father's hand and walk with him to the old butcher's shop, where we would be greeted by clucking from the crates lined up at the entrance. My father always chose the chicken himself. He'd squat down, eyes scanning the birds, looking for the right size – not too big, not too bony. When he pointed, the butcher, Abou Ali, would nod, grab the chicken, and with a swift motion take it to the back where I'd watch in half curiosity, half awe. We'd bring it home fresh in the paper wrap, and my mother would begin the ritual, pounding garlic, squeezing lemons, massaging the marinade into every part of the bird. By early afternoon, the charcoal was lit. My father stood over the barbecue, turning the chicken slowly as the smoke curled up into the trees. It was a dish for garden lunches, family gatherings, and Sunday barbecues – always eaten hot, straight off the grill, with khobez, toum, and loud voices around the table.

Start by cleaning the chicken well with cold water. Rub with a little salt and lemon juice, rinse again, then pat fully dry with clean kitchen towels.

In a deep bowl, mix the olive oil, lemon juice, grated garlic, pepper paste, vinegar, Baharat, salt, black pepper, and paprika together. Whisk until smooth. The marinade should be bold, garlicky, and vibrant in colour.

Place the chicken in a tray or large resealable bag. Pour the marinade over it, turning and rubbing it thoroughly into the meat and under the skin. Let the chicken marinate, covered, in the fridge for at least 6 hours or ideally overnight.

Bring the marinated chicken to room temperature before cooking. Grill over hot charcoal, turning every few minutes and basting with the leftover marinade. Start skin-side down, but finish skin-side up to get a deep char without burning the chicken.

Alternatively, roast the chicken in a preheated oven at 220°C (200°C fan) for 45–50 minutes, then grill on high for 5–10 minutes to brown and crisp the skin.

Rest the cooked chicken for 10 minutes before serving. Cut into quarters or halves and serve with toum (see page 203), pickles, fries, and warm khobez.

Lahmé Meshwiyé
لحم مشوي

Tender lamb skewers, flame-grilled the
Lebanese way
Serves 4–5

For the lahmé meshwiyé

1kg lamb or beef rump

4 tbsp olive oil

1 tbsp apple cider vinegar

1 tbsp plain full-fat yoghurt

½ tbsp pepper paste or tomato paste

1 tbsp Baharat (Lebanese 7 spices)

1 tbsp sumac

1 tsp fine sea salt, or to taste

½ tsp freshly ground black pepper

For the téblé salad

2 large red onions, finely sliced

1 large bunch fresh flat-leaf parsley, finely
chopped

¼ bunch fresh mint, leaves picked

2 tsp sumac

½ tsp fine sea salt, or to taste

1 tbsp extra virgin olive oil

Juice of 1 lemon

Notes...

If grilling over charcoal, soak wooden
skewers in water for 30 minutes before use.

Leftover lahmé can be wrapped in khobez for
a quick snack the next day (see the sandwiché
recipe on page 164).

Lahmé meshwiyé is a beloved dish that captures the spirit
of Lebanese street food and home cooking alike. In the
bustling streets of Beirut, it's common to find traditional
butchery shops grilling tender, marinated meat skewers
right outside their doors. The smoky aroma of sizzling
lamb and beef fills the air, mingling with the sounds and
sights of the city. These freshly grilled meats are often
served wrapped in warm khobez as simple yet irresistible
sandwiches, enjoyed by locals and visitors on the go. This
sensory experience, the scent of charred meat and spices
drifting through the streets, is part of what makes lahmé
meshwiyé so deeply woven into Lebanese culture. For me,
it recalls childhood memories of street vendors and family
gatherings, where the thrill of smoky, juicy meat fresh from
the grill was always a cause for celebration.

To prepare and cook the skewers

Start by trimming the meat of any excess fat, leaving a thin layer to
add flavour and juiciness. Cut into even cubes of about 40–45g each
and then place the meat in a large, clean bowl.

In a separate bowl, combine all the remaining ingredients and whisk
thoroughly until well blended. Pour this marinade over the meat and
fold gently to coat every piece completely. Cover the bowl tightly and
refrigerate for at least 6 hours, preferably overnight, allowing the
spices to penetrate and tenderise the meat.

When ready to cook, remove the meat from the refrigerator and
bring it to room temperature. Thread the meat onto soaked wooden
skewers, leaving space between pieces for even cooking.

Grill the skewers over a hot charcoal grill or preheated grill pan at
medium-high heat, turning frequently. Cook for approximately 12–15
minutes, until the meat is nicely charred on the outside and cooked to
your preferred doneness on the inside.

To prepare the salad and serve

While the meat is cooking, prepare the téblé salad by combining
the finely sliced onion, chopped parsley and mint leaves in a bowl.
Sprinkle with the sumac and fine sea salt, then drizzle with the olive
oil and lemon juice. Toss gently to mix and let the flavours marry.

Serve the grilled meat skewers immediately with warm khobez, grilled
baby onions and tomatoes, and the fresh téblé salad. A side of toum
(see page 203) or pomegranate molasses will elevate the flavours
even further.

Samke Meshwiyé
سمكة مشوية

Grilled fish with tarator & smoky
aubergine salad
Serves 4–5

2 whole white fish such as sea bass, sea
bream, or snapper, approx. 700–800g
each

6 garlic cloves, finely grated

Juice of 2 lemons

Zest of 1 lemon

4–5 tbsp olive oil

1 tbsp fine sea salt, or to taste

1 tsp freshly ground black pepper

1 tsp ground cumin

1 tsp sumac, for sprinkling

Lemon wedges, for serving

For the tarator
See the recipe on page 202

For the salatet raheb
(smoky aubergine salad)
2 large aubergines

2 spring onions, finely sliced

2 tbsp chopped fresh parsley

1 tbsp chopped fresh mint

Seeds of ½ pomegranate

1 tbsp pomegranate molasses

1 tsp sumac

Juice of 1 lemon

2 tbsp extra virgin olive oil

½ tsp fine sea salt, or to taste

Back in Lebanon during the war, going to the seaside
wasn't just hanging out – it was a small rebellion. Me and
my friends would pile into an old car, windows down,
no destination planned, just the sea calling. We'd stop
by the fish market to pick up whatever fresh fish was left,
sometimes barely enough for everyone. The grill was a
patch of charcoal we'd light wherever we could, often
near the shore. The smoky aubergines, the sharp tarator,
squeezing lemons over everything – it was more than food.
It was freedom, laughter, and a break from all the noise and
fear. Those nights by the fire, eating with dirty hands and
salty air, that's what we lived for.

Clean the fish thoroughly, rinse under cold water, and pat dry.

Mix the garlic, lemon juice, lemon zest, olive oil, salt, pepper, and cumin
together. Rub all over the fish and marinate for 1 hour in the fridge.

Meanwhile, make the tarator according to the recipe on page 202.

Grill the marinated fish whole or filleted over hot charcoal or in a cast-
iron grill pan until the skin is crisp and the flesh flakes easily.

To prepare the salatet raheb
Char the aubergines over an open flame or under a hot grill until
blackened. Peel, drain off any excess liquid, and roughly chop.

Combine the smoky aubergine with the spring onions, parsley, mint,
pomegranate seeds and molasses, sumac, lemon juice, olive oil, and
salt. Stir gently to combine.

Serve the grilled fish sprinkled with sumac alongside the tarator,
salatet raheb, and lemon wedges.

Kreidis Meshwé
قريديس مشوي

Chargrilled tiger prawns glazed in tangy chilli sauce
Serves 4–5

1kg medium-large tiger prawns, cleaned and deveined (shells on or off, as preferred)

1½ tbsp fresh homemade Debs el Harr (see page 194)

5 garlic cloves, finely grated

4 tbsp extra virgin olive oil

2 tbsp fresh lemon juice

Zest of 1 lemon

1 tbsp fine sea salt, or to taste

½ tsp freshly ground black pepper

1 tsp ground cumin

Lemon wedges, to serve

1 tbsp finely chopped fresh parsley (optional)

Tiger prawns from the Eastern Mediterranean shores – caught along the Lebanese coast near Tyre, Batroun and Saida – are prized for their sweet, firm meat. Marinated in fresh homemade Debs el Harr, a Lebanese chilli paste, and extra virgin olive oil, these prawns become smoky, spicy, and perfectly charred on the grill.

First, prepare the Debs el Harr according to the recipe on page 194.

Pat the tiger prawns dry. In a bowl, combine the Debs el Harr, garlic, extra virgin olive oil, lemon juice, lemon zest, salt, black pepper, and cumin. Toss the prawns thoroughly in this marinade, ensuring each one is coated. Cover and refrigerate for 30 minutes.

Preheat the grill to medium-high heat. Thread the marinated prawns on skewers or grill directly on the grates. Grill for 2–3 minutes per side, until the prawns turn pink, opaque, and have a slight char. Avoid overcooking to keep them tender.

Serve hot with lemon wedges and a sprinkle of fresh parsley on top.

Shish Taouk
شيش طاووق

Classic Lebanese chicken skewers,
grilled to smoky perfection
Serves 4–5

1kg chicken breast fillets

250g plain full-fat yoghurt

Juice of 2 large lemons

6 large garlic cloves, finely grated

2 tbsp pepper paste or tomato paste

1 tbsp Baharat (Lebanese 7 spices)

1 tbsp apple cider vinegar

1 tsp smoked paprika

1 tsp fine sea salt, or to taste

1 tsp freshly ground black pepper

2 tbsp pomegranate molasses

5–6 tbsp extra virgin olive oil

A beloved staple of Lebanese grilling culture, shish taouk is all about tenderness, flavour, and balance. The marinade – rich with yoghurt, lemon, garlic, and Baharat – transforms humble chicken into something truly celebratory. Across Lebanon, this dish marks weekends, feasts, and gatherings. In my home, it meant summer lunches in the garden with warm khobez, toum, and a table full of mezza. The scent alone brings me straight back to those long, sunny afternoons.

Begin by rinsing the chicken under cold water, patting it dry with kitchen paper, and trimming off any excess fat. Cut the chicken into 40–45g cubes and place in a clean, dry bowl. In a separate bowl, whisk all the remaining ingredients together until smooth.

Add the chicken to the marinade and fold gently to coat all the pieces thoroughly. Cover tightly with cling film and refrigerate for at least 6 hours, preferably overnight, to develop deep flavour throughout the meat.

When ready to cook, bring the chicken to room temperature. Thread the pieces onto soaked wooden skewers, leaving a little space between each piece for even cooking.

For grilling, preheat a grill or barbecue to medium-high heat and cook the skewers for 12–15 minutes, turning them regularly until the chicken is cooked through and nicely charred on the edges.

Alternatively, preheat your oven to 220°C (200°C fan). Place the skewers on a lightly oiled baking tray or grill rack and roast for 20–25 minutes, turning halfway through for even browning. Ensure the chicken reaches an internal temperature of 75°C and the juices run clear.

Place the skewers on warm khobez and serve with toum (see page 203) and cucumber pickles (see page 198) alongside fresh fries or a tabbouleh salad.

Notes...

If grilling over charcoal, soak wooden skewers in water for 30 minutes before use.

Leftover shish taouk can be wrapped in khobez for a quick snack the next day (see the sandwiché recipe on page 175).

Sandwiché

Wrapped in memory, rolled in khobez

In Lebanon, a sandwich is the taste of break time at school, a midnight snack from the neighbourhood shop, or that quick bite on the beach after a swim. It's a rolled-up moment of home, love, and comfort inside one big piece of Lebanese khobez.

Wherever you go in Lebanon – from the streets of Beirut to the mountains of the Chouf, from Saida's souks to Tripoli's snack bars – everyone knows how to build a proper Lebanese sandwich. There's an art to it. You start with khobez and only khobez. No pita pockets. No wraps. No tortillas. Just the soft, chewy, thin, round Lebanese bread that folds like memory and holds everything together.

Lay the khobez open, maybe doubling up the bread if the filling is juicy. Spread the hummus or the garlic sauce or the labneh with the back of a spoon. Add the main event – kafta, shish, chicken liver, or even leftover batata harra – and then come the extras: crunchy pickles, fresh mint, juicy tomatoes, and crisp lettuce or freshly made fries (yes, fries in the sandwich). Then you roll it up, with purpose, with confidence, tightly but not too tight, so it doesn't tear the bread but still holds the fillings snugly. Wrap it in paper or foil and take a bite – perfection.

For me, and for so many Lebanese, sandwiches are one of our most democratic and delicious pleasures. Rich or poor, young or old, we all love a good sandwiché. There's no ego, no plating, no garnish – just honest food wrapped in honest bread, eaten with your hands, and full of soul. This chapter is a tribute to those moments: the roadside snack bars with their tiny grills and massive flavours; the home-packed school sandwiches made in a rush but with care; the beach sandwiches eaten with wet hair and sandy feet.

These are the sandwiches that fed our childhoods and shaped our tastebuds. And they're still with us, wherever we go.

Let's roll.

Sandwichét Hummus

ساندويش حمص

Street-style creamy hummus sandwich
Serves 4

4 large Lebanese khobez

400g creamy hummus (see the recipe on page 80)

8–10 radishes, thinly sliced

4 spring onions, finely chopped

120g turnip pickles, cut into thin strips

Small handful of fresh mint leaves, torn

1 tsp smoked paprika, or to taste

Fine sea salt, to taste

Drizzle of extra virgin olive oil

When money was tight, or time was short, this was our go-to. A scoop of hummus, topped with whatever was fresh from the fridge, wrapped in warm khobez – no fuss, but full of life. I still remember sitting on the balcony with my older sister, unwrapping the sandwich from newspaper, eating it slowly while watching the street below. This is the kind of sandwich you can eat on the go, in a schoolyard, or with a glass of tea on a lunch break. It's humble, but it hits the spot every time. Classic, simple and deeply satisfying.

Lay out the khobez. Spread each one with a generous layer of hummus. Top with the sliced radish, spring onion, pickles, fresh mint, and a sprinkle of smoked paprika.

Season lightly with sea salt and finish with a drizzle of olive oil if desired. Roll up tightly from the bottom, folding the sides in as you go to keep the filling secure.

Serve the wrap with tomato slices sprinkled with sumac and extra virgin olive oil on the side if you like.

Sandwichét
Shawarma Lahmé
ساندويش شاورما لحم

Beef shawarma with tarator & sumac
téblé salad
Serves 4

For the beef shawarma
600g beef sirloin or flank steak, thinly
sliced

1 medium brown onion, thinly sliced

1 small orange, deseeded and very finely
diced (peel and pulp)

½ lemon, deseeded and very finely diced
(peel and pulp)

2 tbsp tomato or pepper paste (biber
salçası or similar)

3 tbsp apple cider vinegar

4 tbsp olive oil

1 tsp fine sea salt, or to taste

1 tsp Baharat (Lebanese 7 spices)

½ tsp freshly ground black pepper

¼ tsp ground cardamom

Pinch of grated nutmeg

For the sumac téblé salad
See the recipe on page 153

To assemble
4 large Lebanese khobez

8 tbsp tarator (see page 202)

200g turnip pickles, sliced into strips

1 tomato, thinly sliced

If there's one sandwich that defines Lebanese street food, it's shawarma. Wrapped fast by hands that have done it a thousand times – it's not just lunch, it's a ritual. In Beirut, it's the midnight fix after a night out, the quick bite between errands, or the reason you take a longer route home that passes your favourite shawarma guy. The scent alone – warm spices, roasting beef, the tang of pickles and tarator – pulls you across the street. What makes Lebanese shawarma different from other grilled meat wraps like döner and gyros? It's thinner, bolder, cleaner – no heavy sauces, no extra filler. Just spiced meat, punchy condiments and the perfect khobez wrap, done with balance and precision. This is Beirut's unbeatable bite.

To prepare the beef shawarma
In a large bowl, combine all the ingredients except the beef to make a marinade. Add the thinly sliced beef and rub well so the spices and citrus coat the meat thoroughly. Cover and refrigerate for at least 4 hours, preferably overnight, to marinate.

To roast the shawarma, preheat your oven to 200°C (220°C fan) and spread the marinated beef on a lined tray. Roast for 15–20 minutes, turning once.

To pan-sear the shawarma, heat a heavy pan with drizzle of olive oil and cook the marinated beef in batches until browned and caramelised.

To assemble
Warm the khobez. Spread each one with two generous spoonfuls of tarator, add the hot beef shawarma, then top with the pickles and sliced tomato. Roll up tightly from the bottom, folding in the sides as you go to keep the filling secure. If you like, wrap in parchment paper and toast lightly in a pan or sandwich press until the bread is golden, lightly crisp and warm. Serve with fries or a cold Almaza and thank me later.

Notes...
The diced citrus peel gives this marinade a Beirut-style edge – sweet, sharp and fragrant.

Tarator should be zingy and garlicky. Loosen the consistency with cold water until it drizzles smoothly.

Turnip pickles are essential – they cut through the richness and add crunch.

BEIRUT
BEIRUT

Sandwichét Shawarma Djej

ساندويش شاورما دجاج

Spiced chicken shawarma with fries,
pickles & toum
Serves 4

For the chicken

1 lemon, deseeded and finely diced (peel
and pulp)

6 large garlic cloves, finely grated

3 tbsp olive oil

3 tbsp lemon juice

2 tbsp apple cider vinegar

1 tbsp pomegranate molasses

1 tbsp pepper paste

1½ tsp Baharat (Lebanese 7 spices)

1 tsp sumac

1 tsp smoked paprika

1 tsp fine sea salt, or to taste

½ tsp freshly ground black pepper

600g boneless, skinless chicken thighs,
thinly sliced

To assemble

4 large Lebanese khobez

100g toum (see page 203)

1 large Maris Piper or chipping potato,
peeled and cut into thin fries

Rapeseed oil, for frying

OR replace the fries with a handful of
shredded lettuce

80g cucumber pickles, cut into strips

Before the war scattered our family across the world, my older siblings and I had a little ritual. When things in Beirut felt a bit safer, even just for a moment, they'd take me to Hamra for a sandwich at Barbar. That buzzing corner of the city never slept, and their shawarma was the kind that stuck with you – the aroma, the heat of the wrap in your hands, the sharpness of the garlicky toum against the spiced chicken, the salty pickles, and the crunch of that first bite into hot fries. It was fast food, yes – but for us, it was a treat and a moment of rare peace.

In a large bowl, combine all the ingredients for the chicken except the thigh meat, then add the sliced chicken thighs, mix well to coat, cover the bowl, and refrigerate for at least 4–6 hours or overnight.

To cook the chicken in a pan, heat a heavy pan with a drizzle of oil over medium-high heat. Cook the marinated chicken in batches, spreading it out so it browns, not steams. Sear until golden and cooked through, 6–8 minutes in total.

To cook the chicken in the oven, spread the marinated chicken on a lined tray. Roast in a preheated oven at 200°C (180°C fan) for 20–25 minutes, turning once, until golden and slightly crisp at the edges.

If you're making fries, fry the potato in hot oil until golden and crisp. Drain on kitchen paper and season with fine sea salt.

Once your chicken and fries are ready, warm the khobez. Spread each one with toum, add a handful of fries (or crisp lettuce), the chicken shawarma, and pickles. Roll up tightly from the bottom, folding in the sides as you go to keep the filling secure. Wrap in parchment paper and toast lightly in a pan or sandwich press until the bread is golden, lightly crisp and warm. Dip your wrap in more toum for extra flavour.

Sandwichét Ma'aalé
ساندويش مقالي

Fried cauliflower & aubergine sandwich
with creamy mtabbal
Serves 4

4 large Lebanese khobez

6 tbsp aubergine mtabbal (see page 88)

1 aubergine and 1 cauliflower, fried (see
the recipe for Ma'aalé on page 63)

2 ripe tomatoes, sliced

100g cucumber pickles, sliced

4 tsp pomegranate molasses

1 lemon, cut into wedges

A few mint or parsley leaves (optional)

Every Saturday morning, before the city fully woke up, Mum and I would head to the market with our woven bag. She would walk straight to her trusted stall, the one with the cleanest, glossiest small cauliflowers and those perfect baladi aubergines, deep purple with no seeds. She'd gently press each one, checking for firmness, freshness, that little give that told her it was good. I'd trail behind her, secretly hoping we'd stop for a sesame kaak on the way home. Back in our apartment, the frying pan came out. The scent of aubergine and cauliflower crisping in olive oil filled the whole building. When the wraps were ready, every bite tasted like the market, like home, like Beirut.

Warm the khobez slightly so they are soft and flexible. Spread a generous spoonful of aubergine mtabbal across the centre of each one. Layer with a mix of the fried aubergine and cauliflower — they should still be warm and crisp. Add slices of tomato and pickles, drizzle with pomegranate molasses, and give it a good squeeze of fresh lemon juice. Top with fresh herbs if you like.

Roll up tightly from the bottom, folding in the sides as you go to keep the filling secure. You can eat it as is or toast it lightly in a pan or sandwich press until golden and lightly crisp.

Notes...

Dusting the aubergine slices with flour before frying keeps them from soaking up too much oil.

Mtabbal is the heart of this sandwich, bringing creaminess and smokiness.

A few fresh mint leaves elevate the filling for a refreshing twist.

Serve with a glass of laban ayran – that's all you need for the perfect snack or quick lunch.

Sandwichét Beid
w Sumac
ساندويش بيض بالسماق

Scrambled eggs with sumac &
pomegranate molasses
Serves 4

4 tbsp extra virgin olive oil

1 garlic clove, finely grated

6 large free-range eggs

1½ tsp sumac

½ tsp Baharat (Lebanese 7 spices)

Fine sea salt, to taste

Freshly ground black pepper, to taste

4 large Lebanese khobez

2 large vine tomatoes, sliced

4 spring onions, sliced lengthways

Handful of fresh mint leaves, picked

1 tbsp pomegranate molasses, or to taste

Some mornings in Beirut, especially when we were rushing to school or work, Mum would whip up this quick, fragrant, and filling scrambled egg. I remember standing in the kitchen, half asleep, watching her whisk the eggs while garlic sizzled gently in the pan. Then she'd wrap everything in khobez with herbs and fresh veg and hand it to us with a napkin, no plate. That combination of warm egg, tangy molasses, and sharp mint stays with you. It's breakfast, lunch, comfort food and a little act of love, all in one wrap.

Heat the olive oil gently in a non-stick pan. Add the grated garlic and sauté just until fragrant – don't let it brown. Crack in the eggs and stir over medium heat, scrambling them gently. Add the sumac, Baharat, sea salt, and black pepper. Cook until just set but still soft, then remove from the heat.

Lay out each khobez. Spoon the warm scrambled eggs down the centre. Top with sliced tomato, spring onion, and fresh mint. Drizzle lightly with pomegranate molasses. Roll up tightly from the bottom, folding the sides in as you go to keep the filling secure. Serve immediately – these are best eaten warm.

Sandwichét Falafel
ساندويش فلافل

Crispy falafel, turnip pickles & tarator
Serves 4

16 falafel balls (see the recipe on page 91)

4 large Lebanese khobez

8 tbsp tarator (see the recipe on page 202)

2 large ripe tomatoes, chopped

2 small handfuls of fresh mint leaves and chopped parsley

80g turnip pickles, sliced

1 small green chilli or a spoonful of chilli paste (optional)

Crunchy falafel in warm khobez with all the fixings, just like a street stop in Saida. Coming back from our family trips to the South, we had to stop in Saida for a falafel sandwich at the legendary Abou Nabil. Everyone would crowd outside, elbows touching, shouting their order, and waiting for that perfect wrap: hot, crunchy falafel stuffed into warm bread with tarator, pickles, fresh vegetables, and a handful of mint. We'd stand on the pavement, one hand holding the sandwich, the other a little paper cone of turnip pickles and fresh chilli. It was simple, fast, and everything you needed. Vegan, filling, and packed with texture – this is Lebanese street food at its best.

Fry the falafel until golden and crisp – they should be piping hot. Lay the khobez on a clean surface and spread a generous layer of tarator down the centre. Scatter over the chopped tomato, fresh mint and parsley, pickles, and hot falafel balls, crushing them gently with your hand so they sit flat and absorb the sauce. If you like it spicy, add the chilli too. Roll up tightly from the bottom, folding the sides in as you go to keep the filling secure. Serve straight away with chilli pickles on the side.

Notes...

Always fry falafel fresh – they lose their magic if left too long.

Use pink turnip pickles for proper Lebanese sharpness.

The tarator should be silky, lemony, and coat every bite.

Sandwichét Shish Taouk
ساندويش شيش طاووق

Charcoal grilled chicken, toum &
cucumber pickles

Serves 4

500g shish taouk, grilled and cut into
thick strips (see the recipe on page 158)

1 large Maris Piper or chipping potato,
peeled and cut into thin fries

Rapeseed oil, for frying

OR replace the fries with a handful of
shredded lettuce

4 large Lebanese khobez

4 heaped tbsp toum (see page 203)

100–120g cucumber pickles, sliced

In Beirut, you don't ask what's in the shish taouk sandwich, you just know. It's always the same and always perfect: grilled chicken with smoky char, a swipe of sharp toum, crunchy cucumber pickles, and crispy golden fries, all wrapped tightly in warm Lebanese khobez. No tomato. No lettuce. No fuss. This is how it's done at every corner shop from Hamra to Mar Mikhael. As kids, we'd queue up after school, watching the guy behind the counter work like a magician – flipping fries, slathering toum, rolling with speed and precision. The first bite was pure joy.

If you're making fries, fry the potato in hot oil until golden and crisp. Drain on kitchen paper and season with fine sea salt.

Warm the khobez and lay them flat. Spread a tablespoon of toum across the centre of each one. Top with the shish taouk, a handful of fries (or lettuce if you prefer), and pickles.

Roll up tightly from the bottom, folding in the sides as you go to keep the filling secure. Wrap in parchment paper and toast lightly in a pan or sandwich press until the bread is golden, lightly crisp and warm for the real Lebanese experience: juicy, garlicky, and straight from the Beirut snack scene.

Notes...

This is the gold standard of Lebanese wraps, no extras needed.

Add extra toum if you're brave. Be careful if you're on a date.

If you're making a batch of these, wrap and press in a hot pan when they're all ready to serve for a crisp finish.

Sandwichét Kafta
ساندويش كفتة

With hummus, pickles & onion salad
Serves 4

1 small red onion, finely sliced

1 small bunch flat-leaf parsley, finely
chopped (about 20g leaves)

1 tbsp sumac

Juice of ½ lemon

Fine sea salt, to taste

4 large Lebanese khobez

200g creamy hummus (see the recipe on
page 80)

500g kafta, grilled or pan-seared (see the
recipe on page 149)

2 medium vine tomatoes, sliced

120g cucumber pickles, sliced

1 tsp smoked paprika

In Lebanon, the kafta sandwich is more than just a quick meal, it's part of the everyday rhythm of life. Whether it's a family picnic or a quick bite from your favourite neighbourhood snack shop, everyone knows exactly how it should taste – smoky kafta, creamy hummus, sharp pickles, and a punchy onion salad that brings it all together. It's simple, but when wrapped in fresh Lebanese khobez, it becomes something unforgettable.

In a small bowl, mix the sliced onion with the chopped parsley, sumac, lemon juice, and a pinch of salt. Let it sit for a few minutes to soften and marinate.

Lay the khobez flat. Spread a generous spoonful of hummus across the centre. Add a line of kafta, tomato slices, pickles, and a generous spoonful of the onion salad. Season with smoked paprika.

Roll up tightly from the bottom, folding in the sides as you go to keep the filling secure. For extra flavour and texture, wrap in parchment paper and toast lightly in a pan or sandwich press until golden.

Serve your sandwichét with laban ayran – that's how we do it in Beirut.

Notes...

The onion salad brings brightness – don't skip it.

You can use white onion if needed, but red gives better sweetness.

If preparing ahead, wrap in parchment to keep the bread from drying out.

Hélweyét

Sweet memories from the heart of Beirut

Sweetness, for us Lebanese, isn't just about sugar. It's about joy. It's about moments. It's about the quiet comfort of something warm after a long day, or the excitement of visiting someone and being greeted by a tray of baklawa and small cups of Arabic coffee. Our desserts are stories – layered, delicate, and deeply rooted in tradition.

For me, it all started with my dad's pastry shop in Beirut. May he rest in peace. I must have been seven or eight when I began helping out, usually on weekends and after school. He would be up at 5am every morning without fail, the scent of orange blossom and semolina filling the air before the sun even rose. I remember the sound of the metal shutters going up, the quiet hum of the shop coming to life, the trays of cheese knefe already baking in the oven.

By midday, the knefe was sold out. People would queue outside, especially on Sundays. My reward after helping was always the same: one portion of knefe, cut fresh, layered into a sesame kaak roll, warm syrup poured generously over it. I'd sit on the little stool outside the shop, syrup dripping down my fingers and staining my t-shirt, but I didn't care. I was too busy enjoying the stringy cheese, the floral notes of orange blossom, and that feeling of being part of something special.

Even now, whenever I visit Beirut, that memory hits me. One bite of proper knefe and I'm back outside my dad's shop, legs swinging off the stool, sun warming the pavement, and life tasting exactly as it should – sweet.

This chapter is a tribute. To my father. To our traditions. To every Lebanese home where desserts are made with care. From mhalabieh to atayef, nammoura to osmaliyeh, this is how we make hélweyét in Lebanon – properly, proudly, and always with heart.

Osmaliyeh b'Tine
أُصْمَلِيِّة بِتِين

Baked kataifi with orange blossom ashta
& poached figs
Serves 4–5

For the ashta and syrup
See the recipe for Atayef b'ashta on page
185

For the pastry
250g kataifi pastry (shredded filo)
100g unsalted butter, melted

For the poached figs
10–12 small ripe figs, halved
2 tbsp caster sugar
Zest of ½ orange
2 tbsp orange blossom water
150ml water

To serve
Extra syrup
75g crushed pistachios

Osmaliyeh is one of those Lebanese sweets that feels like a celebration – golden, crisp, and delicate. It's the dessert you bring out when family's visiting, or when you want to show off a little. I remember trips with my family up to the mountains during fig season, crates of tender fruit balanced in the boot, orange blossom scent drifting from the glove box. This version honours those memories, using figs gently poached with sugar and citrus to create something soft, sweet, and perfect with a spoon of cold ashta and a good drizzle of syrup.

First, prepare the ashta and syrup according to the recipe on page 185.

Preheat your oven to 180°C (160°C fan). Fluff the kataifi pastry with your hands, pour over the melted butter and mix well. Divide in half and firmly press each portion into a 22cm tart or cake tin to form two even, compact discs around 1.5cm thick. Bake for 18–22 minutes until golden brown. Leave to cool completely.

Place the figs cut side up in a non-stick pan with the sugar, orange zest, and orange blossom water, then pour in the water. Cover and simmer over low heat for 6–8 minutes until softened and syrupy but still holding their shape. Leave to cool.

Place one kataifi disc on a serving tray. Spread the chilled ashta cream over the base. Arrange most of the poached figs gently on top. Place the second kataifi disc over the filling, pressing lightly. Place a small spoonful of ashta in the centre, then drizzle with syrup and garnish with the crushed pistachios. Finish with the remaining poached figs and a little of their poaching syrup, then serve immediately with more syrup on the side.

Notes...

If your figs are very ripe, only poach them briefly – just enough to become perfumed and softened without falling apart.

The kataifi base must be firmly pressed and evenly shaped before baking so it holds without cracking.

Don't rush the assembly – everything must be cool so the cream doesn't melt.

Atayef b'Joz
قطايف بالجوز

Stuffed Lebanese pancakes with walnuts
& cinnamon
Serves 6–8 | Makes about 18–20

For the syrup
See the recipe for Atayef b'ashta on page
185

For the atayef
See the recipe for Atayef b'ashta on page
185
Rapeseed oil, for shallow frying

For the filling
300g walnuts, finely chopped

3 tbsp caster sugar

1½ tsp ground cinnamon

3 tbsp orange blossom water

1 tbsp rose water

For the yoghurt dip
200g full-fat natural yoghurt

2 tbsp strawberry purée (make your own
by blending a few ripe strawberries)

1 tsp rose water

1–2 tsp honey (optional)

Atayef b'Joz is one of the classic desserts of Ramadan, but in our house it was a year-round favourite. My sisters and I would always sneak one or two while they were still warm and sticky with syrup. Unlike the creamy version filled with ashta (see page 185), these are heartier – filled with walnuts, spiced with cinnamon and orange blossom, and folded like half-moons. My father always preferred these, especially with a strong Lebanese coffee after dinner. To lighten them up, I now serve them with a rose and strawberry yoghurt dip which brings freshness to the richness of the filling.

First, prepare your syrup and atayef according to the recipe on page 185.

Next, prepare the filling by mixing the chopped walnuts with the sugar, cinnamon, orange blossom water, and rose water in a bowl. It should be fragrant and just sticky enough to hold together.

Heat a non-stick pan over medium heat. Stir the atayef batter gently and pour small rounds (about 8cm diameter) into the dry pan. Cook on one side without flipping them – bubbles will appear on top, and the surface will set. Set aside on a clean towel and keep covered so they don't dry out.

Place about a heaped teaspoon of the walnut filling in the centre of each pancake. Fold them into half-moons and pinch the edges firmly to seal. Press well so they don't open while frying.

Shallow fry the filled atayef in hot oil until golden and crisp on both sides. Drain on kitchen paper, then immediately dip into or drizzle generously with the cooled syrup.

To make the dip, mix the yoghurt with the strawberry purée, rose water, and honey to taste, if using. Chill for 15 minutes before serving.

Serve the atayef warm with the rose-strawberry yoghurt dip on the side or a small spoonful on top.

Notes...
Make sure the pancakes are sealed tightly before frying.

You can toast the walnuts lightly before making the filling for extra depth.

The yoghurt dip balances the sweetness and adds a lovely floral finish.

Atayef b'Ashta
قطايف بالقشطة

Stuffed Lebanese pancakes with fresh
clotted cream & orange blossom syrup
Serves 6–8 | Makes about 18–20

For the syrup
200g caster sugar

120ml water

1 tbsp lemon juice

1 tbsp rose water

1 tbsp orange blossom water

For the ashta
1.2L whole milk

4 tbsp white vinegar or lemon juice

1½ tbsp cornflour

1 tbsp caster sugar

1 tbsp rose water

2 tbsp orange blossom water

200g ricotta cheese (optional but
recommended)

For the atayef
300g plain flour

1 tsp dried instant yeast

1 tsp caster sugar

1 tsp bicarbonate of soda

Pinch of fine sea salt

100ml whole milk

350–400ml lukewarm water

For the garnish
80g finely chopped pistachios

1 tbsp rose petal jam

Atayef were always a treat we looked forward to – especially around Ramadan or on Sunday afternoons when visitors dropped by unannounced. The smell of the hot saj (pan) as the batter bubbles and sets, the sight of the ashta filling being spooned in generously, the syrup dripping slowly over the soft folds – it's simple, sweet Lebanese hospitality in a bite. We couldn't resist pinching some from the tray before they made it to the guests. My mother always knew, but she let us get away with it.

To prepare the syrup
Combine the sugar and water in a small saucepan. Bring to a boil, then add the lemon juice. Lower the heat and simmer for 8–10 minutes until slightly thickened. Add the rose and orange blossom waters, stir, and then remove from the heat. Cool to room temperature.

To prepare the ashta
In a saucepan, bring 1 litre of the milk to a simmer. Add the vinegar or lemon juice and stir gently until the milk curdles and separates. Strain and discard the whey, keeping the curds.

In a clean saucepan, mix the remaining 200ml of milk with the cornflour and sugar. Stir over medium heat until it thickens to a soft custard. Add the rose and orange blossom waters.

Now mix the custard with the curds and ricotta (if using). Let the ashta cool completely and chill for at least an hour.

To prepare the atayef
In a large bowl, whisk together the flour, yeast, sugar, bicarbonate of soda, and salt. Slowly whisk in the milk and water, adjusting the quantity to get a smooth, pourable batter. Cover and leave to rest for 30–45 minutes until slightly bubbly.

Heat a non-stick pan over medium heat. Stir the batter gently and pour or ladle small rounds (about 8cm diameter) into the dry pan. Cook on one side without flipping them – bubbles will appear on top, and the surface will set. Set aside on a clean towel and keep covered so they don't dry out.

Place about a spoonful of ashta in the centre of each pancake. Fold them into half-moons and pinch one edge firmly to seal, leaving the other edge open so the cream peeks out.

Arrange the atayef on a platter, drizzle with the syrup and sprinkle with chopped pistachios and rose petal jam. Serve immediately or chill lightly before serving.

Nammoura
نمورة مع فواكه

Sticky semolina cake with macerated plums
Serves 6–8

Nammoura was often on the table back home – a soft, sticky, golden cake dotted with almonds. I've made it my way this time, with macerated plums like the ones my mum used to soak in sugar on the balcony. Their syrup sinks into the cake, sharp and sweet – it's still the same comforting treat, just with a bit more of me in it.

For the syrup

250g caster sugar

180ml water

1 tsp lemon juice

2 tsp orange blossom water

2 tsp rose water

For the macerated fruit

4 ripe red plums, quartered

80g pomegranate seeds

1 tbsp caster sugar or clear honey

Zest and juice of 1 orange

1 tsp orange blossom water

1 tsp rose water

For the nammoura

200g coarse semolina

100g fine semolina

100g grated coconut

150g caster sugar

1 tsp bicarbonate of soda

½ tsp baking powder

Pinch of fine sea salt

200g full-fat plain yoghurt

100g unsalted butter, melted

3 tbsp orange blossom water

3–4 tbsp water

Whole blanched almonds

To prepare the syrup

Combine the sugar and water in a small saucepan. Bring to a boil, then add the lemon juice. Lower the heat and simmer for 8–10 minutes until slightly thickened. Add the orange blossom and rose waters, stir, and then remove from the heat. Cool to room temperature.

To prepare the macerated fruit

Toss the quartered plums and pomegranate seeds in a bowl with the sugar or honey, orange zest, orange juice, and orange blossom and rose waters. Cover and set aside for at least 30–45 minutes.

To prepare the nammoura

In a large bowl, mix both types of semolina with the coconut, sugar, bicarbonate of soda, baking powder, salt, and yoghurt. Pour in the melted butter, orange blossom water, and water. Stir well until everything is combined and the texture is smooth with no lumps.

Pour the batter into a greased 25cm square or round baking dish. Smooth the top. Let it rest for 15–20 minutes at room temperature.

Score the surface lightly into squares or diamonds. Place one whole almond in the centre of each piece. Bake in a preheated oven at 180°C fan for 30–35 minutes, or until golden and set. Move to the top rack and cook for another 10–15 minutes for a deeper colour (watch it carefully).

As soon as the nammoura comes out of the oven, pour the cooled syrup evenly over the hot cake. Let it soak for 1–1.5 hours before serving.

Slice into squares or diamonds, following the score lines you made earlier. Spoon the macerated fruit generously over each portion just before serving.

Notes...

Let the nammoura fully absorb the syrup before serving – patience is key.

For a deeper nuttiness to the flavour, toast the coconut before mixing in.

You can swap red plums for sour cherries or poached quince in winter.

Mhalabieh
مهلبية

Lebanese chilled milk pudding with grenadine
Serves 4–5

1 litre full-fat milk

100g caster sugar

80g cornflour

100g double cream

3 tbsp rose water

3 tbsp orange blossom water

80ml grenadine syrup (good quality, ideally natural pomegranate based)

Crushed pistachios

Dried rose petals (optional)

There was always a tray of mhalabieh in the fridge, tucked behind the water jug or a bowl of olives, waiting to be spooned into small bowls after lunch. My sister liked hers with just crushed pistachios, but I always went for the pink one – topped with a swirl of grenadine. That delicate ripple of colour and flavour, sweet and slightly sharp, made it feel special. This version is just like those days of my childhood: simple, comforting, and quietly beautiful.

Pour 800ml of the milk into a saucepan with the sugar. In a bowl, whisk the remaining 200ml of milk with the cornflour until completely dissolved. Slowly add the cornflour mix into the warm milk, stirring constantly over medium heat.

Keep stirring gently until the mixture thickens, about 10–12 minutes over low heat, then add the double cream and stir for about 5 minutes. The cream gives it body and texture – the mixture should coat the back of a spoon at this stage.

Turn off the heat and stir in the rose and orange blossom waters. Pour the mhalabieh into serving glasses or shallow bowls and set aside to cool slightly. Drizzle the grenadine gently on top to create a thin layer. Refrigerate for at least 3 hours or until fully set.

Garnish the puddings with crushed pistachios and a few rose petals if you like. Serve chilled.

Knefe b'Jibneh
كنافة بالجبنة

Warm sweet cheese & crispy kataifi pastry
Serves 4–5

For the cheese filling
400g Akkawi cheese

150g full-fat mozzarella, grated

1 tbsp fine semolina

1 tbsp caster sugar

For the syrup
250g caster sugar

125ml water

1 tsp lemon juice

1 tbsp orange blossom water

1 tsp rose water

For the kataifi
300g kataifi pastry (shredded filo),
thawed if frozen

90g samneh or unsalted butter, melted

To serve
Pistachios, to garnish (optional)

Sesame kaak or Lebanese khobez

In Lebanon, knefe isn't just dessert – it's breakfast, celebration, memory, and pride. For me, it will always be the scent of my father's pastry shop early in the morning, the hiss of melted cheese on the burner, the steam from the syrup pot, the trays cooling on marble counters. In my father's shop, trays were flipped just before the morning call to prayer, sending clouds of steam and the scent of orange blossom into the street. This version is the original – no shortcuts, no extra layers – and that first bite, warm and dripping with syrup, is still unbeatable.

To prepare the cheese
Soak the Akkawi in cold water for at least 6–8 hours or overnight, changing the water several times to remove excess salt. Drain, pat dry, and grate. Combine with the grated mozzarella.

To prepare the syrup
Combine the sugar, water and lemon juice in a small saucepan. Bring to a gentle boil, skim off any impurities, then lower the heat and simmer for 8–10 minutes until lightly thickened. Remove from the heat, then stir in the orange blossom and rose waters. Set aside to cool completely.

To prepare the kataifi
Using clean hands, separate and loosen the kataifi pastry into fine threads. Pour over the melted samneh and rub gently until every strand is coated. Spread half of the kataifi evenly into a greased 25cm round baking dish, pressing firmly to form a compact base.

To prepare the filling, assemble and bake
Preheat the oven to 180°C. Mix the grated cheeses with the semolina and sugar. Spread this evenly over the kataifi base. Cover with the remaining kataifi, pressing gently but not too firmly. Bake in the preheated oven for 30–35 minutes, until the top is crisp and golden.

Remove from the oven and immediately pour the cooled syrup evenly over the hot knefe. Allow to rest for 5–10 minutes so the syrup is absorbed, then garnish with pistachios if desired.

Serve hot, cut into squares or scooped directly into warm sesame kaak, as is tradition, or Lebanese khobez.

Notes...
Don't skip pressing the base well – this creates the clean, professional finish.

Toasted sesame kaak bread (similar to bagels) can be substituted with khobez for the sandwich version of this delicious dessert.

Namlieh

The heart of the home

Every Lebanese home had a namlieh, what you might call a pantry, that old wooden cupboard with its wire-mesh doors guarding jars of love and patience. Inside were the colours and scents of our seasons: fig jam, thick and golden from the summer sun, wild za'atar gathered from the hills, ruby-red sumac glowing through old glass jars, and awarma sealed in fat to see us through the winter. Among the shelves stood bright jars of kabiss – pickled cucumbers, turnips, and wild cauliflower – adding a sharp, joyful note to every meal.

The namlieh was more than storage; it was memory. It held our mothers' hands, our grandmothers' secrets, and the rhythm of home-cooked life. Each jar and bottle told a story of family, of resourcefulness, and of the quiet pride in making something from what the land offered.

EXTRA VIRGIN OLIVE OIL
SAIFAN

Debs el Harr
دبس الحرّ

The chilli sauce that speaks for itself
Makes 1 small jar

150g fresh long red chillies, deseeded
and roughly chopped

4 garlic cloves, peeled

1 tsp fine sea salt, or to taste

1 tsp sugar (optional)

1 tsp ground cumin

1 tbsp pepper paste

60ml extra virgin olive oil

20ml apple cider vinegar

Every Lebanese family have their own version of Debs el Harr, and no two are exactly the same, but one thing is certain – there's always a jar of it in the fridge. Whether it's used to fire up a plate of mdardara, spooned onto grilled tiger prawns (kreidis) or stirred into labneh to be scooped up with warm bread, this chilli sauce is more than a condiment – it's part of how we eat.

The name literally means 'molasses of heat' which says everything – it's bold, sharp, deep, spicy, and slightly sweet when it wants to be. In our house, someone was always blending up fresh red chillies, garlic, vinegar, and olive oil, tasting, adjusting, adding just a little more lemon. You learn by instinct. And it's never measured exactly – it's felt.

I make mine with fresh red chillies (choose the type depending on the season – long and bright, not too bitter), garlic, apple cider vinegar, extra virgin olive oil, pepper paste, and seasoning. That's it. But quality matters. Always use the best olive oil you have and fresh, firm chillies (not the wilted soft ones). It should be spicy, yes, but balanced. Not just heat for the sake of it.

It keeps beautifully, the kind of thing you make once and enjoy for weeks. I store it in a glass jar, always topped with a thin layer of oil to preserve the flavour. In time, the sharpness mellows a little, but the depth stays. And somehow, even a small spoonful makes a dish come alive. I serve it with arnabit (fried cauliflower), samke harra, kibbé, or honestly, just with warm flatbread and nothing else. It's that good.

Blend the chillies, garlic, salt, sugar (if using) and cumin until smooth but slightly coarse. Add the pepper paste and blend briefly, then gradually add the olive oil and apple cider vinegar while blending to form a thick, spreadable paste. Taste and adjust the seasoning if needed.

Store the paste in a clean jar. Press down to remove air bubbles, cover the surface with a thin layer of extra virgin olive oil, seal tightly, and refrigerate. Use within 3 weeks, always with a clean spoon.

Kabiss Arnabit
كبيس قرنبيط

Lebanese pickled cauliflower
Makes 1.5 litres (2 large jars)

1 small cauliflower (about 1kg)

1 small raw beetroot, peeled

3 garlic cloves, peeled

1L water

3 tbsp coarse sea salt or kosher salt

200ml distilled or white wine vinegar

1 small red chilli (optional, for a bit of heat)

2 x 750ml sterilised glass jars

In Lebanon, when cauliflower starts to show up in every souk stall, snowy white heads furled in pale green leaves, you know pickling season is in full swing. My mum always bought the clean, tightly packed, smaller heads to be chopped into florets and set in brine with beetroot to give the pickle that pink hue we all loved. Crisp, sour kabiss arnabit would be waiting on the side of nearly every winter meal – and just like kabiss léfét, it's a must with grilled meat, falafel, or in a sandwich with hummus and mint.

Start by trimming your cauliflower into florets – the smaller and more evenly sized they are, the faster and more evenly they'll pickle. Give them a good rinse and set aside. Slice the beetroot into thick rounds and crush the garlic cloves.

In a clean saucepan, bring the water to a boil. Add the salt and stir until it's completely dissolved. Remove from the heat and pour in the vinegar. Allow the brine to cool completely to room temperature – this step is essential for keeping the cauliflower crisp.

Now, start layering your jars. Add a few slices of beetroot to the bottom of each jar, followed by cauliflower florets, a clove of garlic, and if you like, a piece of red chilli. Repeat until the jars are full but not packed too tight – leave space for the brine to circulate.

Pour the cooled brine into the jars, covering their contents completely. Gently tap the jars on a flat surface to release any air bubbles and then seal them tightly.

Let the jars sit in a cool, dark place or in the fridge for 5–7 days. The beetroot will slowly infuse the cauliflower with its beautiful pink hue. Once the pickled florets are tangy and crunchy, they're ready to enjoy. Keep the jars in the fridge after opening and they'll last a month or more.

Notes...

Always use fresh, firm cauliflower with no soft spots or green patches.

Don't rush the pickling process – it needs time for the flavour and colour to develop.

Want a more intense pink? Add a few more beetroot slices to your jars.

Kabiss Khyar
كبيس خيار

Lebanese pickled cucumbers
Makes 1.5 litres (2 large jars)

1kg small Lebanese or Persian cucumbers

1L water

3 tbsp coarse sea salt or kosher salt

200ml distilled or white wine vinegar

6 garlic cloves, peeled and lightly crushed

1–2 small red chillies (optional)

A few sprigs of fresh dill (optional)

2 x 750ml sterilised glass jars

No Lebanese meal feels quite complete without a bowl of crunchy, salty, tangy pickled cucumbers sitting proudly on the table. Every home, every balcony kitchen, every Sunday lunch has its version. My mother's kabiss was always just right – never too sharp, never too soft and always ready when the table was full. She'd prepare the jars after her morning coffee, stacking cucumbers neatly while the brine cooled. Sometimes she'd tuck in a fresh chilli or a sprig of dill, and we'd sneak a bite long before they were ready. This is her recipe, unchanged, just as we all remember it.

Start by preparing your cucumbers (the smaller and firmer, the better). Give them a good wash, dry them thoroughly, and trim off the stalk tips if needed, but keep their shape intact. Meanwhile, prepare your brine. Bring the water to a boil, stir in the sea salt until it dissolves completely, then take off the heat and stir in the vinegar. Let this cool to room temperature.

Into the bottom of each clean jar, drop a few crushed garlic cloves, a red chilli if you're adding heat, and a sprig of fresh dill if you like that herby fragrance. Stack the cucumbers in snugly, upright if they fit, making sure to fill the jar without bruising them.

Slowly pour the cooled brine into the jars, covering their contents completely. Gently tap the jars on a flat surface to release any air bubbles and then seal them tightly.

Let the jars sit in a cool, dark place or in the fridge for 5–7 days, or up to 10 days if you like your pickles sharper. Once opened, keep them in the fridge and enjoy them cold, straight from the jar, with grilled meats, in sandwiches, or simply with bread and labneh. They'll keep beautifully for a few weeks, but they never last long in our house.

Notes...

Pickling is one of those things we do instinctively in Lebanon – it's not just about preserving, it's about always having something on hand to wake up a meal. Just like good bread or olive oil, kabiss is part of the rhythm of the kitchen. Keep it simple, keep it clean, and let time do the rest.

Kabiss Léfét
كبيس لفت

Lebanese pickled turnips
Makes 1.5 litres (2 large jars)

1kg fresh, firm, small or medium white turnips

1 small raw beetroot

4 garlic cloves

1L water

3 tbsp coarse sea salt or kosher salt

200ml distilled or white wine vinegar

1 small red chilli (optional, for a kick)

2 x 750ml sterilised glass jars

There's nothing like the crunch and bold pink colour of kabiss léfét to make a plate of shawarma, falafel, or grilled meat complete. I can still see my mum slicing the turnips on a Sunday afternoon, her hands stained slightly pink from the beetroot, preparing the brine like she always did, from memory. In every Lebanese home, these pickles live in the fridge or on the balcony, soaking up flavour and bringing brightness to any bite. Sour, salty, and a little earthy, they're a must.

Begin with good, firm turnips — the whiter and crunchier, the better. Give them a good scrub and peel, then slice them into thick wedges or batons, not too thin, so they hold their crunch, but small enough to pickle evenly.

Peel and slice the beetroot into thick rounds — just one is enough, as it's here for colour more than flavour, adding that beautiful blush that makes this pickle iconic. Peel and crush the garlic cloves.

Now prepare the brine. Bring the water to a boil, stir in the sea salt until it dissolves completely, then take off the heat and stir in the vinegar. Let this cool to room temperature — hot brine would soften the turnips too much, and we want that signature snap.

In your clean glass jars, layer the turnips with a couple of beetroot slices, some garlic, and, if you like, a little chilli for heat. Repeat the layering until the jars are nearly full. Slowly pour the cooled brine into the jars, covering their contents completely. Gently tap the jars on a flat surface to release any air bubbles and then seal them tightly.

Let the jars sit in a cool, dark place or in the fridge for 7–10 days. The beetroot will slowly release its colour, turning everything a vibrant pink. Once they've reached your preferred level of sharpness, they're ready. Keep the jars in the fridge after opening and they'll last a month or more.

Tarator
طرطور

Not just 'tahini sauce'
Serves 6–8

200g tahini
Juice of 1 large lemon
Juice of 1 medium orange
3 large garlic cloves, finely grated
Pinch of fine sea salt, or to taste
80–100ml cold water

In Lebanon, we don't call it tahini sauce – we call it tarator. Tahini is just the base, the sesame paste. But when it's whisked with lemon juice, garlic, water, and a pinch of salt, it becomes tarator – a creamy, tangy, bold sauce that somehow tastes like everything good about our food.

It's the quiet hero of so many Lebanese classics. We drizzle it over falafel, spoon it onto crispy fried cauliflower (arnabit), pair it with fish like samke harra or grilled prawns, and serve it alongside kafta. It's never the loudest thing on the plate but take it away and the whole dish falls flat. That's the power of tarator – it lifts, it balances, it brings everything together.

But here's the thing, not all tahini is created equal. The quality of your tahini will make or break your tarator. I've tasted tahini from different countries, some too bitter, some too thick, others far too oily or bland. A good tahini should be smooth, creamy, and fragrant, without a pool of oil floating on top. If the oil is too split or the paste feels grainy or too dry, it won't emulsify well, and your sauce will suffer.

For me, it's always Lebanese tahini – El Yemen & Sons or Al Kanater. That's what I grew up with, and it's what I still use at home and in the restaurant. It gives the sauce the richness and balance it needs – the kind of flavour that doesn't need fixing or hiding.

Making tarator is simple, but it's also something you learn by feel. Add the lemon little by little. Crush the garlic properly. Whisk until it loosens and turns pale and velvety. Taste it, always. It should be bold but never overpowering. When it's right, you'll know.

Tarator isn't fancy or showy. But it's part of us – the way za'atar is part of us, or olive oil, or flatbread still warm from the oven. It's the kind of thing you don't think about much… until it's missing. And then you realise how much it matters.

Whisk the tahini, lemon juice, orange juice, grated garlic, and salt together, then drizzle in the cold water and continue to whisk until you have a smooth and pourable sauce.

Toum
توم

Lebanese garlic sauce
Makes about 250ml

50g large garlic cloves, peeled and lightly crushed

½ tsp fine sea salt, or to taste

200–250ml rapeseed oil

7–8 ice cubes (to keep the mixture cold during emulsification)

2 tbsp freshly squeezed lemon juice

Toum is more than just a sauce, it's a powerful symbol of Lebanese hospitality and bold flavours. For generations, families across Lebanon have prepared this creamy, velvety garlic emulsion to accompany grilled meats, fried foods, and mezza. Its name simply means garlic, but its impact on the palate is profound – a punch of fresh, pungent garlic softened by lemon and oil, creating a sauce that is both fiery and smooth.

Though humble in ingredients, toum holds a special place at every Lebanese table. It evokes memories of lively family gatherings, outdoor barbecues, and the joyful chaos of shared meals. My mother's kitchen was always filled with the aroma of crushed garlic and fresh lemon, as she patiently emulsified toum with care and pride.

In recent years, toum's popularity has spread far beyond Lebanon's borders, captivating food lovers worldwide. Its addictive garlic flavour and creamy texture have made it a sought-after condiment in restaurants and home kitchens alike, from gourmet shawarma joints in London to fusion food trucks in New York. It has been embraced as a versatile sauce, celebrated not only for its taste but for its connection to tradition and community.

True, authentic toum is a simple yet perfect balance of just four ingredients. No additives, no shortcuts. This purity is what makes it so special, allowing the garlic to shine bright and the sauce to develop its unique creamy texture through patient emulsification.

Place the garlic cloves and salt into a food processor with about 50ml of the oil. Pulse until the garlic is finely minced and a smooth paste is formed, scraping down the sides regularly.

Open the processor, add the ice and then very slowly add the remaining rapeseed oil in a thin, steady stream while blending, allowing the mixture to emulsify fully before adding more oil.

Add the lemon juice and continue slowly adding oil until the sauce is thick, creamy, and fluffy. The final texture should be smooth and easily spreadable but firm enough to hold its shape.

Taste and adjust with more salt or lemon juice as desired. Store in an airtight container in the fridge. Always serve chilled.

Notes...

Use the freshest garlic you can find – old or sprouting garlic will affect the flavour and texture.

Adding oil too quickly or blending too fast can cause the sauce to split – patience is key.

Rapeseed oil's mild flavour makes toum lighter, while ice makes it fluffier and prevents the processor from warming which could cause the sauce to split.

A Note on the Recipes

Unless otherwise specified in the recipe, oven temperatures refer to a fan oven, so for a conventional oven you may need to increase the temperature by up to 20°C and adjust the cooking times accordingly.

My Recommendations

As a chef and a father, when I cook for my family – especially for my children – I want to use ingredients that I trust completely. The brands I share here are the same ones we rely on in Lebanon and across the Middle East – not just for their quality, but because they respect the traditions of our cuisine. These are the flavours I grew up with and the ones I pass on to my children. When making these recipes at home, I always tell people: use the best you can find. Good olive oil, real tahini, proper pomegranate molasses – these small choices bring the heart of Lebanese cooking to life in your kitchen. In the UK, many of these trusted brands are now easy to find in Middle Eastern shops and online – they will serve you well.

When buying dried chickpeas, try to find the larger sized ones (preferably 9mm to 12mm) as these have the best texture and flavour.

Baharat – Abido

brown burghul – Gardenia or Durra

extra virgin olive oil – Zejd, Al Wadi, Terroirs du Liban, Koura Premium, Mymouné or Zaytoun

freekeh – Gardenia

ful medammas – California Garden or Cortas

halloum cheese – Cortas, Cedar, or Milky's

kishek powder – Chtoura or Al Rabih

Lebanese khobez – Dina Foods or Rayan

Lebanese za'atar blend – Mymouné, Cortas or Abido

mloukhieh – Gardenia

moghrabieh – Gardenia or Durra

orange blossom and rose water – Mymouné, Cortas or Chtoura

pepper paste – Oncü

pomegranate molasses – Al Wadi, Al Kanater, Cortas or Al Rabih

sumac – Sofra or Terroirs du Liban

Glossary

arghileh – similar to a hookah or shisha pipe, for smoking flavoured tobacco

ashta – creamy filling for Lebanese pastries, similar to clotted cream

baa'leh – purslane, edible plant whose leaves and stems can be eaten raw or cooked

Baharat – Lebanese blend of seven spices

Békaa – valley in eastern Lebanon

djej – chicken

Fairouz – celebrated Lebanese singer

Habibi – darling or my love, always used informally

hummus – dish made with chickpeas, tahini and olive oil

kabiss khyar – pickled cucumber

kabiss léfét – pickled turnip

kafta – spiced minced meat

khobez – Lebanese flatbread

kibbet / kibbé / kibbeh – potato dish whose name varies according to context

laban – fresh natural yoghurt mixed with salt and ice, served as a drink or side dish

lahém or lahmé – red meat

manou'sheh – singular form of mana'eesh, Lebanese flatbreads baked with toppings

markouk – unleavened Lebanese flatbread, a thin village bread made on the Saj

méshwi – grilled

mezza – traditional spread of many dishes that brings everyone together

namlieh – pantry

sajiyyeh – traditional Lebanese clay or cast-iron cooking pot

samneh – organic clarified butter, similar to ghee

shankleesh – tangy cheese made from strained and fermented yoghurt

shay bil naa'naa' – black tea infused with fresh mint

shorba or shorbét – Lebanese soup

tarator – tahini-based sauce with lemon and garlic, often eaten with falafel and fish

téh'wijé – blend of herbs and spices, particular to individual families

Teta – grandmother

toum – garlic sauce, often eaten with grilled meats

za'atar barri – wild thyme

A

Akkawi cheese

Mana'eesh Jibneh (Baked halloumi & Akkawi cheese flatbread) 39

Knefe b'Jibneh (Warm sweet cheese & crispy kataifi pastry) 190

Aleppo pepper / Aleppo chilli flakes

Balila (Chickpeas, olive oil & lemon broth) 28

Mana'eesh Za'atar (Baked wild thyme, sumac & sesame flatbread) 35

Mana'eesh Banadoura (Baked tomato, onion, sumac & olive oil flatbread) 41

Lahém b'Ajine (Golden baked flatbread with spiced minced lamb) 43

Kibbet Batata (Mashed potato kibbé with burghul, herbs & onions) 56

Salatet Halloum w Battikh (Grilled halloumi salad with watermelon, mint & olive oil) 71

Hummus Beiruti (Smoky, herby, garlicky hummus — the Beirut way) 85

Lebanese Muhammara (Smoky, spicy roasted red pepper, walnut & olive oil dip) 86

Batata Harra (Crunchy potatoes sizzling with garlic, coriander & chilli) 99

Samke Harra (Spiced baked fish with tarator, pine nuts & coriander) 117

Almaza beer

Sandwichét Shawarma Lahmé (Beef shawarma with tarator & sumac téblé salad) 164

Almonds

Freekeh b'Lahmé (Smoky roasted green wheat with lamb, sultanas & toasted nuts) 110

Burghul w Djej (Nutty burghul cooked in broth with tender chicken) 136

Nammoura (Sticky semolina cake with macerated plums) 186

Arak

Sawda Ghanam (Lamb livers seared with garlic, lemon & Baharat) 50

Fraké Nayyé (Southern-style spiced lamb tartare) 53

Salatet Halloum w Battikh (Grilled halloumi salad with watermelon, mint & olive oil) 71

Ashta

Atayef b'Ashta (Stuffed Lebanese pancakes with fresh clotted cream & orange blossom syrup) 185

Aubergine

Ma'aalé (Lebanon's favourite fried vegetables with tarator & pomegranate) 63

Baba Ghanouj (Smoky aubergine salad) 83

Mtabbal Batenjen (Creamy, garlicky, smoky: the real Lebanese mtabbal) 88

Maghmour (Lebanon's moussaka: aubergine baked with chickpeas, tomato & olive oil) 122

Sheikh el Mehshi (Baked baby aubergines stuffed with spiced mince in rich tomato sauce) 135

Samké Meshwiyé (Grilled fish with tarator & smoky aubergine salad) 154

Sandwichét Ma'aalé (Fried cauliflower & aubergine sandwich with creamy mtabbal) 168

B

Baa'leh (purslane)

Salatet Shamandar (Sweet, salty, crunchy beetroot, feta & walnut salad) 96

Salatet Fattoush (Lebanon's signature salad: colourful vegetables, crisp khobez & bright sumac) 100

Baharat (Lebanese 7 spices)

E'jjeh (Lebanese herby egg fritters) 31

Beid w Awarma (Lebanese eggs with preserved lamb confit & pomegranate molasses) 32

Lahém b'Ajine (Golden baked flatbread with spiced minced lamb) 43

Shorbet Djej with Vermicelli (Soothing Lebanese chicken & vermicelli soup) 46

Sawda Ghanam (Lamb livers seared with garlic, lemon & Baharat) 50

Shorbet Mawzet (Lebanon's winter soup: lamb shank, rice & rich broth) 59

Loubieh b Zeit (Flat green beans simmered in tomatoes, garlic & olive oil) 60

Batata w Beid (Pan-fried potatoes & eggs with olive oil & Baharat) 67

Sawda Djej (Caramelised chicken livers with garlic, lemon & pomegranate molasses) 72

Khadija's Tabbouleh (The beginning of every gathering: my mum's tabbouleh) 92

Arayes (Grilled Lebanese khobez stuffed with spiced minced lamb) 105

Freekeh b'Lahmé (Smoky roasted green wheat with lamb, sultanas & toasted nuts) 110

Bemieh b'Lahmé (Slow-cooked baby okra & lamb stew) 113

Djej b'Sayniyeh (Tray-baked chicken with potatoes, garlic, lemon & coriander) 114

Fasoulia b'Lahmé (A hearty pot of butter beans & lamb, slowly simmered for deep flavour) 118

Kafta b'Sayniyeh (Kafta, potato & tomato traybake) 121

Bazella b'Lahmé (Lebanese-style lamb, peas & carrots in hearty tomato sauce) 125

Réz b'Dfine (Fragrant rice with tender oxtail, cooked in rich broth) 127

Sélée Mehshi (Stuffed chard leaves with rice, mince & lemony broth) 132

Sheikh el Mehshi (Baked baby aubergines stuffed with spiced mince in rich tomato sauce) 135

Burghul w Djej (Nutty burghul cooked in broth with tender chicken) 136

Moghrabieh (Semolina pearls, spiced chicken & onions in caraway-scented sauce) 138

Jawaneh Meshwi (Chicken wings with garlic, coriander, lemon & chilli) 144

Kastaleta (Lamb chops grilled over hot coals, marinated in garlic, lemon & Baharat) 147

Kafta Meshwiyé (Charcoal-grilled minced meat skewers with tarator & téblé salad) 149

Farrouj Meshwé (Charcoal-grilled spatchcock chicken with toum & fries) 150

Lahmé Meshwiyé (Tender lamb skewers, flame-grilled the Lebanese way) 153

Shish Taouk (Classic Lebanese chicken skewers, grilled to smoky perfection) 158

Sandwichét Shawarma Lahmé (Beef shawarma with tarator & sumac téblé salad) 164

Sandwichét Shawarma Djej (Spiced chicken shawarma with fries, pickles & toum) 167

Sandwichét Beid w Sumac (Scrambled eggs with sumac & pomegranate molasses) 171

Beef

Arayes (Grilled Lebanese khobez stuffed with spiced minced lamb) 105

Bazella b'Lahmé (Lebanese-style lamb, peas & carrots in hearty tomato sauce) 125

Sélée Mehshi (Stuffed chard leaves with rice, mince & lemony broth) 132

Sheikh el Mehshi (Baked baby aubergines stuffed with spiced mince in rich tomato sauce) 135

Kafta Meshwiyé (Charcoal-grilled minced meat skewers with tarator & téblé salad) 149

Lahmé Meshwiyé (Tender lamb skewers, flame-grilled the Lebanese way) 153

Sandwichét Shawarma Lahmé (Beef shawarma with tarator & sumac téblé salad) 164

Used as a substitute:

Lahém b'Ajine (Golden baked flatbread with spiced minced lamb) 43

Bemieh b'Lahmé (Slow-cooked baby okra & lamb stew) 113

Beef, minced

Arayes (Grilled Lebanese khobez stuffed with spiced minced lamb) 105

Kafta Meshwiyé (Charcoal-grilled minced meat skewers with tarator & téblé salad) 149

Beef rump

Lahmé Meshwiyé (Tender lamb skewers, flame-grilled the Lebanese way) 153

Beef sirloin

Sandwichét Shawarma Lahmé (Beef shawarma with tarator & sumac téblé salad) 164

Beetroot

Salatet Shamandar (Sweet, salty, crunchy beetroot, feta & walnut salad) 96

Kabiss Arnabit (Lebanese pickled cauliflower) 197

Kabiss Léfét (Lebanese pickled turnips) 201

Bell pepper

Lebanese Muhammara (Smoky, spicy roasted red pepper, walnut & olive oil dip) 86

Salatet Fattoush (Lebanon's signature salad: colourful vegetables, crisp khobez & bright sumac) 100

Bemieh (okra)

Bemieh b'Lahmé (Slow-cooked baby okra & lamb stew) 113

Black tea

Mana'eesh Jibneh (Baked halloumi & Akkawi cheese flatbread) 39

Broad beans, dried

Falafel (Saida-Style: The taste of Saida's souk) 91

Bulgur/Burghul

Mana'eesh Kishek (Baked fermented yoghurt & burghul flatbread) 36

Kibbet Banadoura (Juicy tomato kibbé from the south of Lebanon) 54

Kibbet Batata (Mashed potato kibbé with burghul, herbs & onions) 56

Mjaddara Hamra (Brown lentils & burghul with smoky onions: the pride of the South) 64

Khadija's Tabbouleh (The beginning of every gathering: my mum's tabbouleh) 92

Burghul w Djej (Nutty burghul cooked in broth with tender chicken) 136

Butter beans
Fasoulia b'Lahmé (A hearty pot of butter beans & lamb, slowly simmered for deep flavour) 118

C

Carrots
Shorbet Mawzet (Lebanon's winter soup: lamb shank, rice & rich broth) 59
Bazella b'Lahmé (Lebanese-style lamb, peas & carrots in hearty tomato sauce) 125

Cauliflower
Ma'aalé (Lebanon's favourite fried vegetables with tarator & pomegranate) 63
Sandwichét Ma'aalé (Fried cauliflower & aubergine sandwich with creamy mtabbal) 168
Kabiss Arnabit (Lebanese pickled cauliflower) 197

Celery
Used as a substitute:
Shorbet Djej with Vermicelli (Soothing Lebanese chicken & vermicelli soup) 46
Shorbet Mawzet (Lebanon's winter soup: lamb shank, rice & rich broth) 59

Chicken, whole
Shorbet Djej with Vermicelli (Soothing Lebanese chicken & vermicelli soup) 46
Djej b'Sayniyeh (Tray-baked chicken with potatoes, garlic, lemon & coriander) 114
Mloukhieh (Earthy jute mallow with tender chicken in a fragrant broth) 131
Burghul w Djej (Nutty burghul cooked in broth with tender chicken) 136
Moghrabieh (Semolina pearls, spiced chicken & onions in caraway-scented sauce) 138
Farrouj Meshwé (Charcoal-grilled spatchcock chicken with toum & fries) 150

Chicken breast
Shish Taouk (Classic Lebanese chicken skewers, grilled to smoky perfection) 158
Sandwichét Shish Taouk (Charcoal grilled chicken, toum & cucumber pickles) 175

Chicken livers
Sawda Djej (Caramelised chicken livers with garlic, lemon & pomegranate molasses) 72

Chicken thighs
Sandwichét Shawarma Djej (Spiced chicken shawarma with fries, pickles & toum) 167

Chicken wings
Jawaneh Meshwi (Chicken wings with garlic, coriander, lemon & chilli) 144

Chickpeas, dried
Balila (Chickpeas, olive oil & lemon broth) 28
Hummus Beiruti (Smoky, herby, garlicky hummus — the Beirut way) 85
Saida-Style Falafel (The taste of Saida's souk, freshly fried and drizzled with tahini) 91
Maghmour (Lebanon's moussaka: aubergine baked with chickpeas, tomato & olive oil) 122

Chickpeas, cooked/jarred
Ful w Hummus (Creamy fava beans & chickpeas mashed with garlic, lemon & olive oil: the king of breakfast) 24
Balila (Chickpeas, olive oil & lemon broth) 28
Maghmour (Lebanon's moussaka: aubergine baked with chickpeas, tomato & olive oil) 122
Réz b'Dfine (Fragrant rice with tender oxtail, cooked in rich broth) 127
Burghul w Djej (Nutty burghul cooked in broth with tender chicken) 136
Moghrabieh (Semolina pearls, spiced chicken & onions in caraway-scented sauce) 138

Chicory
Hindbeh b Zeit (Sautéed wild dandelion greens with caramelised onions) 75

Chilli, fresh (red/green)
Ful w hummus (Creamy fava beans & chickpeas mashed with garlic, lemon & olive oil: the king of breakfast) 24
Mana'eesh Kishek (Baked fermented yoghurt & burghul flatbread) 36
Sawda Ghanam (Lamb livers seared with garlic, lemon & Baharat) 50
Fraké Nayyé (Southern-style spiced lamb tartare) 53
Kibbet Banadoura (Juicy tomato kibbé from the south of Lebanon) 54
Kibbet Batata (Mashed potato kibbé with burghul, herbs & onions) 56

Hummus Beiruti (Smoky, herby, garlicky hummus — the Beirut way) 85
Lebanese Muhammara (Smoky, spicy roasted red pepper, walnut & olive oil dip) 86
Zeitoun Mchakkal (Lebanese marinated green & black olives) 106
Samke Harra (Spiced baked fish with tarator, pine nuts & coriander) 117
Jawaneh Meshwi (Chicken wings with garlic, coriander, lemon & chilli) 144
Sandwichét Falafel (Crispy falafel, turnip pickles & tarator) 172
Debs el Harr (The chilli sauce that speaks for itself) 194
Kabiss Arnabit (Lebanese pickled cauliflower) 197
Kabiss Khyar (optional) (Lebanese pickled cucumbers) 198
Kabiss Léfét (optional) (Lebanese pickled turnips) 201

Chilli paste
Sandwichét Falafel (Crispy falafel, turnip pickles & tarator) 172

Chilli pickles
Maghmour (Lebanon's moussaka: aubergine baked with chickpeas, tomato & olive oil) 122
Sandwichét Falafel (Crispy falafel, turnip pickles & tarator) 172

Coconut, grated
Nammoura (Sticky semolina cake with macerated plums) 186

Courgette
Ma'aalé (Lebanon's favourite fried vegetables with tarator & pomegranate) 63

Cucumber
Salatet Banadoura (tomato and cucumber salad - served with Ma'aalé) 63
Laban b'Khyar (yoghurt with cucumber - served with Mjaddara Hamra) 64
Salatet Fattoush (Lebanon's signature salad: colourful vegetables, crisp khobez & bright sumac) 100
Kabiss Khyar (Lebanese pickled cucumbers) 198

Cucumber pickles
Sandwichét Shawarma Djej (Spiced chicken shawarma marinade) 167
Sandwichét Ma'aalé (Fried cauliflower & aubergine sandwich with creamy mtabbal) 168
Sandwichét Shish Taouk (Charcoal grilled chicken, toum & cucumber pickles) 175
Sandwichét Kafta (With hummus, pickles & onion salad) 176

D

Dandelion Greens
Hindbeh b Zeit (Sautéed wild dandelion greens with caramelised onions) 75

Debs el Harr (Lebanese chilli sauce)
Kreidis Meshwé (Chargrilled tiger prawns glazed in tangy chilli sauce) 157

E

Eggs
Beid w Banadoura (Lebanese-style eggs with fresh tomatoes & olive oil) 27
E'jjeh (Lebanese herby egg fritters) 31
Beid w Awarma (Lebanese eggs with preserved lamb confit & pomegranate molasses) 32
Batata w Beid (Pan-fried potatoes & eggs with olive oil & Baharat) 67
Sandwichét Beid w Sumac (Scrambled eggs with sumac & pomegranate molasses) 171

F

Falafel
Falafel (Saida-Style: The taste of Saida's souk, freshly fried and drizzled with tahini) 91
Sandwichét Falafel (Crispy falafel, turnip pickles & tarator) 172

Fava beans, cooked
Ful w hummus (Creamy fava beans & chickpeas mashed with garlic, lemon & olive oil: the king of breakfast) 24

Fava beans, fresh
Ful Maa'la Akhdar (Green fava beans with garlic, coriander & lemon: the taste of early spring) 68

Feta cheese
Salatet Shamandar (Sweet, salty, crunchy beetroot, feta & walnut salad) 96

Figs
Osmaliyeh b'Tine (Baked kataifi with orange blossom ashta & poached figs) 181

Freekeh (roasted green wheat)
Freekeh b'Lahmé (Smoky roasted green wheat with lamb, sultanas & toasted nuts) 110

Ful medammas (cooked fava beans)
Ful w Hummus (Creamy fava beans & chickpeas mashed with garlic, lemon & olive oil: the king of breakfast) 24

G

Green beans, flat
Loubieh b Zeit (Flat green beans simmered in tomatoes, garlic & olive oil) 60

Grenadine syrup
Mhalabieh (Lebanese chilled milk pudding with grenadine) 189

H

Halloumi cheese
Mana'eesh Jibneh (Baked halloumi & Akkawi cheese flatbread) 39
Salatet Halloum w Battikh (Grilled halloumi salad with watermelon, mint & olive oil) 71

Honey
Atayef b'Joz (yoghurt dip) 182
Nammoura (macerated fruit) 186

K

Kafta (Spiced minced meat)
Kafta b'Sayniyeh (Kafta, potato & tomato traybake) 121
Kafta Meshwiyé (Charcoal-grilled minced meat skewers with tarator & téblé salad) 149
Sandwichét Kafta (With hummus, pickles & onion salad) 176

Kataifi pastry (shredded filo)
Osmaliyeh b'Tine (Baked kataifi with orange blossom ashta & poached figs) 181
Knefe b'Jibneh (Warm sweet cheese & crispy kataifi pastry) 190

Khobez (Lebanese flatbread)
Ful w hummus (Creamy fava beans & chickpeas mashed with garlic, lemon & olive oil: the king of breakfast) 24
Fraké Nayyé (Southern-style spiced lamb tartare) 53
Ful Maa'la Akhdar (Green fava beans with garlic, coriander & lemon: the taste of early spring) 68
Hindbeh b Zeit (Sautéed wild dandelion greens with caramelised onions) 75
Mdardara (Hearty green lentils & rice with caramelised onions) 76
Salatet Fattoush (Lebanon's signature salad: colourful vegetables, crisp khobez & bright sumac) 100
Arayes (Grilled Lebanese khobez stuffed with spiced minced lamb) 105
Maghmour (Lebanon's moussaka: aubergine baked with chickpeas, tomato & olive oil) 122
Mloukhieh (Earthy jute mallow with tender chicken in a fragrant broth) 131
Sandwichét Hummus (Street-style creamy hummus sandwich) 163

Sandwichét Shawarma Lahmé (Beef shawarma with tarator & sumac téblé salad) 164
Sandwichét Shawarma Djej (Spiced chicken shawarma with fries, pickles & toum) 167
Sandwichét Ma'aalé (Fried cauliflower & aubergine sandwich with creamy mtabbal) 168
Sandwichét Beid w Sumac (Scrambled eggs with sumac & pomegranate molasses) 171
Sandwichét Falafel (Crispy falafel, turnip pickles & tarator) 172
Sandwichét Shish Taouk (Charcoal grilled chicken, toum & cucumber pickles) 175
Sandwichét Kafta (With hummus, pickles & onion salad) 176
Knefe b'Jibneh (for serving/sandwich version) 190

Kishek powder (fermented yoghurt & burghul)
Mana'eesh Kishek (Baked fermented yoghurt & burghul flatbread) 36

L

Laban
Laban b'Khyar (yoghurt with cucumber dip – served with Mjaddara Hamra) 64

Labneh (strained yoghurt)
Labneh Mtawwameh (Garlicky labneh dip) 88

Lamb
Beid w Awarma (Lebanese eggs with preserved lamb confit) 32
Fraké Nayyé (Southern-style spiced lamb tartare) 53
Shorbet Mawzet (Lebanon's winter soup: lamb shank, rice & rich broth) 59
Arayes (Grilled Lebanese khobez stuffed with spiced minced lamb) 105
Freekeh b'Lahmé (Smoky roasted green wheat with lamb, sultanas & toasted nuts) 110
Bemieh b'Lahmé (Slow-cooked baby okra & lamb stew) 113
Fasoulia b'Lahmé (A hearty pot of butter beans & lamb, slowly simmered for deep flavour) 118
Bazella b'Lahmé (Lebanese-style lamb, peas & carrots in hearty tomato sauce) 125
Sélée Mehshi (Stuffed chard leaves with rice, mince & lemony broth) 132
Sheikh el Mehshi (Baked baby aubergines stuffed with spiced mince in rich tomato sauce) 135
Kastaleta (Lamb chops grilled over hot coals, marinated in garlic, lemon & Baharat) 147
Kafta Meshwiyé (Charcoal-grilled minced meat skewers with tarator & téblé salad) 149
Lahmé Meshwiyé (Tender lamb skewers, flame-grilled the Lebanese way) 153

Lamb chops
Kastaleta (Lamb chops grilled over hot coals, marinated in garlic, lemon & Baharat) 147

Lamb confit
Beid w Awarma (Lebanese eggs with preserved lamb confit) 32

Lamb leg
Beid w Awarma (Lebanese eggs with preserved lamb confit) 32
Fraké Nayyé (Southern-style spiced lamb tartare) 53

Lamb livers
Sawda Ghanam (Lamb livers seared with garlic, lemon & Baharat) 50

Lamb, minced
Lahém b'Ajine (Golden baked flatbread with spiced minced lamb) 43
Arayes (Grilled Lebanese khobez stuffed with spiced minced lamb) 105

Lamb shank
Shorbet Mawzet (Lebanon's winter soup: lamb shank, rice & rich broth) 59

Lamb shoulder
Beid w Awarma (Lebanese eggs with preserved lamb confit) 32
Fraké Nayyé (Southern-style spiced lamb tartare) 53

Freekeh b'Lahmé (Smoky roasted green wheat with lamb, sultanas & toasted nuts) 110
Bemieh b'Lahmé (Slow-cooked baby okra & lamb stew) 113
Fasoulia b'Lahmé (A hearty pot of butter beans & lamb, slowly simmered for deep flavour) 118
Bazella b'Lahmé (Lebanese-style lamb, peas & carrots in hearty tomato sauce) 125
Sélée Mehshi (Stuffed chard leaves with rice, mince & lemony broth) 132
Sheikh el Mehshi (Baked baby aubergines stuffed with spiced mince in rich tomato sauce) 135
Kafta Meshwiyé (Charcoal-grilled minced meat skewers with tarator & téblé salad) 149

Lamb stew
Bemieh b'Lahmé (Slow-cooked baby okra & lamb stew) 113

Lentils, brown
Mjaddara Hamra (Brown lentils & burghul with smoky onions: the pride of the South) 64

Lentils, green
Adass bil Hamod (Lemony green lentil & Swiss chard soup) 49
Mdardara (Hearty green lentils & rice with caramelised onions) 76

Lettuce, romaine
Khadija's Tabbouleh (for serving - scooping the salad) 92
Salatet Fattoush (Lebanon's signature salad) 100

M

Mloukhieh (dried jute mallow leaves)
Mloukhieh (Earthy jute mallow with tender chicken in a fragrant broth) 131

Mozzarella cheese
Knefe b'Jibneh (Warm sweet cheese & crispy kataifi pastry) 190

O

Okra
Bemieh b'Lahmé (Slow-cooked baby okra & lamb stew) 113

Olives
Mana'eesh Jibneh (Baked halloumi & Akkawi cheese flatbread) 39
Hindbeh b Zeit (Sautéed wild dandelion greens with caramelised onions) 75
Salatet l'Batata (Fluffy potatoes dressed in lemon, olive oil & pomegranate) 102
Zeitoun Mchakkal (Lebanese marinated green & black olives) 106

Onions, baby
Moghrabieh (Semolina pearls, spiced chicken & onions in caraway-scented sauce) 138

Onions, red
Téblé salad (served with Lahmé Meshwiyé) 153
Sandwichét Kafta (With hummus, pickles & onion salad) 176

Onions, spring
Ful w hummus (Creamy fava beans & chickpeas mashed with garlic, lemon & olive oil: the king of breakfast) 24
E'jjeh (Lebanese herby egg fritters) 31
Fraké Nayyé (Southern-style spiced lamb tartare) 53
Batata w Beid (Pan-fried potatoes & eggs) 67
Baba Ghanouj (Smoky aubergine salad) 83
Khadija's Tabbouleh (The beginning of every gathering: my mum's tabbouleh) 92
Salatet Shamandar (Sweet, salty, crunchy beetroot, feta & walnut salad) 96
Salatet Fattoush (Lebanon's signature salad: colourful vegetables, crisp khobez & bright sumac) 100
Salatet l'Batata (Fluffy potatoes dressed in lemon, olive oil & pomegranate) 102
Samké Meshwiyé (Grilled fish with tarator & smoky aubergine salad) 154
Sandwichét Hummus (Street-style creamy hummus sandwich) 163
Sandwichét Beid w Sumac (Scrambled eggs with sumac & pomegranate molasses) 171

Orange, whole
Sandwichét Shawarma Lahmé (Beef shawarma with tarator & sumac téblé salad) 164

Orange, zest & juice
Osmaliyeh b'Tine (Baked kataifi with orange blossom ashta & poached figs) 181
Nammoura (Sticky semolina cake with macerated plums) 186
Tarator (Not just 'tahini sauce') 202

Orange blossom water
Osmaliyeh b'Tine (Baked kataifi with orange blossom ashta & poached figs) 181
Atayef b'Joz (Stuffed Lebanese pancakes with walnuts & cinnamon) 182
Atayef b'Ashta (Stuffed Lebanese pancakes with fresh clotted cream & orange blossom syrup) 185
Nammoura (Sticky semolina cake with macerated plums) 186
Mhalabieh (Lebanese chilled milk pudding with grenadine) 189
Knefe b'Jibneh (Warm sweet cheese & crispy kataifi pastry) 190

Oxtail
Réz b'Dfine (Fragrant rice with tender oxtail, cooked in rich broth) 127

P

Peas
Bazella b'Lahmé (Lebanese-style lamb, peas & carrots in hearty tomato sauce) 125

Pine nuts
Freekeh b'Lahmé (Smoky roasted green wheat with lamb) 110
Samke Harra (Spiced baked fish with tarator) 117
Sheikh el Mehshi (Baked baby aubergines stuffed with spiced mince) 135
Burghul w Djej (Nutty burghul cooked in broth with tender chicken) 136

Pistachios
Freekeh b'Lahmé (Smoky roasted green wheat with lamb, sultanas & toasted nuts) 110
Moghrabieh (Semolina pearls, spiced chicken & onions in caraway-scented sauce) 138
Osmaliyeh b'Tine (Baked kataifi with orange blossom ashta & poached figs) 181
Atayef b'Ashta (Stuffed Lebanese pancakes with fresh clotted cream & orange blossom syrup) 185
Mhalabieh (Lebanese chilled milk pudding with grenadine) 189
Knefe b'Jibneh (Warm sweet cheese & crispy kataifi pastry) 190

Plums
Nammoura (Sticky semolina cake with macerated plums) 186

Pomegranate molasses
Beid w Awarma (Lebanese eggs with preserved lamb confit) 32
Mana'eesh Banadoura (Baked tomato, onion, sumac flatbread) 41
Lahém b'Ajine (Golden baked flatbread with spiced minced lamb) 43
Salatet Halloum w Battikh (Grilled halloumi salad with watermelon) 71
Sawda Djej (Caramelised chicken livers with garlic, lemon & pomegranate molasses) 72
Lebanese Muhammara (Smoky, spicy roasted red pepper, walnut & olive oil dip) 86
Fatayer b'Sbenegh (Golden pastry parcels with tangy spinach & onion filling) 95
Salatet Shamandar (Sweet, salty, crunchy beetroot, feta & walnut salad) 96
Salatet l'Batata (Fluffy potatoes dressed in lemon, olive oil & pomegranate) 102
Arayes (Grilled Lebanese khobez stuffed with spiced minced lamb) 105
Kastaleta (Lamb chops grilled over hot coals) 147
Samké Meshwiyé (Grilled fish with tarator & smoky aubergine salad) 154
Shish Taouk (Classic Lebanese chicken skewers grilled to smoky perfection) 158
Sandwichét Ma'aalé (Fried cauliflower & aubergine sandwich with creamy mtabbal) 168
Sandwichét Beid w Sumac (Scrambled eggs with sumac & pomegranate molasses) 171

Pomegranate seeds
Ma'aalé (Lebanon's favourite fried vegetables with tarator & pomegranate) 63
Baba Ghanouj (Smoky aubergine salad) 83
Mtabbal Batenjen (Creamy, garlicky, smoky: the real Lebanese mtabbal) 88
Salatet Shamandar (Sweet, salty, crunchy beetroot, feta & walnut salad) 96
Salatet Fattoush (Lebanon's signature salad: colourful vegetables, crisp khobez & bright sumac) 100

Salatet l'Batata (Fluffy potatoes dressed in lemon & olive oil) 102
Samke Harra (Spiced baked fish with tarator, pine nuts & coriander) 117
Samké Meshwiyé (Grilled fish with tarator & smoky aubergine salad) 154
Nammoura (Sticky semolina cake with macerated plums) 186

Potato

Adass bil Hamod (Lemony green lentil & Swiss chard soup) 49
Kibbet Batata (Mashed potato kibbé with burghul, herbs & onions) 56
Batata w Beid (Pan-fried potatoes & eggs with olive oil & Baharat) 67
Batata Harra (Crunchy potatoes sizzling with garlic, coriander & chilli) 99
Salatet l'Batata (Fluffy potatoes dressed in lemon, olive oil & pomegranate) 102
Djej b'Sayniyeh (Tray-baked chicken with potatoes, garlic, lemon & coriander) 114
Kafta b'Sayniyeh (Kafta, potato & tomato traybake) 121
Sélée Mehshi (Stuffed chard leaves with rice, mince & lemony broth) 132
Sandwichét Shawarma Djej (Spiced chicken shawarma with fries, pickles & toum) 167
Sandwichét Shish Taouk (Charcoal grilled chicken, toum & cucumber pickles) 175

Prawns, tiger

Kreidis Meshwé (Chargrilled tiger prawns glazed in tangy chilli sauce) 157

Purslane (baa'leh)

Salatet Shamandar (Sweet, salty, crunchy beetroot, feta & walnut salad) 96
Salatet Fattoush (Lebanon's signature salad: colourful vegetables, crisp khobez & bright sumac) 100

R

Radish

Ful w Hummus (Creamy fava beans & chickpeas mashed with garlic, lemon & olive oil) 24
Fraké Nayyé (Southern-style spiced lamb tartare) 53
Salatet Fattoush (Lebanon's signature salad: colourful vegetables, crisp khobez & bright sumac) 100
Sandwichét Hummus (Street-style creamy hummus sandwich) 163

Rice, basmati/long grain

Mdardara (Hearty green lentils & rice with caramelised onions) 76
Réz m'Falfal (Lebanese rice with vermicelli) 126
Réz b'Dfine (Fragrant rice with tender oxtail) 127

Rice, short grain

Shorbet Mawzet (Lebanon's winter soup: lamb shank, rice & rich broth) 59
Sélée Mehshi (Stuffed chard leaves with rice & mince) 132

Ricotta cheese

Atayef b'Ashta (Stuffed Lebanese pancakes with fresh clotted cream & orange blossom syrup) 185

Rose petal jam

Atayef b'Ashta (Stuffed Lebanese pancakes with fresh clotted cream & orange blossom syrup) 185

Rose petals, dried

Kibbet Banadoura (Juicy tomato kibbé from the south of Lebanon) 54
Mhalabieh (Lebanese chilled milk pudding with grenadine) 189

Rose water

Atayef b'Joz (Stuffed Lebanese pancakes with walnuts & cinnamon) 182
Atayef b'Ashta (Stuffed Lebanese pancakes with fresh clotted cream & orange blossom syrup) 185
Nammoura (Sticky semolina cake with macerated plums) 186
Mhalabieh (Lebanese chilled milk pudding with grenadine) 189
Knefe b'Jibneh (Warm sweet cheese & crispy kataifi pastry) 190

S

Samneh (Lebanese clarified butter/ghee)

Beid w Awarma (Lebanese eggs with preserved lamb confit & pomegranate molasses) 32
Shorbet Djej with Vermicelli (Soothing Lebanese chicken & vermicelli soup) 46
Freekeh b'Lahmé (Smoky roasted green wheat with lamb) 110
Bemieh b'Lahmé (Slow-cooked baby okra & lamb stew) 113
Réz m'Falfal (Lebanese rice with vermicelli) 126
Réz b'Dfine (Fragrant rice with tender oxtail , cooked in rich broth) 127
Burghul w Djej (Nutty burghul cooked in broth with tender chicken) 136
Moghrabieh (Semolina pearls, spiced chicken & onions) 138
Knefe b'Jibneh (Warm sweet cheese & crispy kataifi pastry) 190

Sea bass/bream

Samke Harra (Spiced baked fish with tarator, pine nuts & coriander) 117
Samké Meshwiyé (Grilled fish with tarator & smoky aubergine salad) 154

Semolina

Nammoura (Sticky semolina cake with macerated plums) 186
Knefe b'Jibneh (Warm sweet cheese & crispy kataifi pastry) 190

Sesame seeds

Za'atar blend (Baked wild thyme, sumac & sesame flatbread) 35
Mana'eesh Jibneh (Baked halloumi & Akkawi cheese flatbread) 39
Salatet Halloum w Battikh (Grilled halloumi salad with watermelon, mint & olive oil) 71
Saida-Style Falafel (The taste of Saida's souk, freshly fried and drizzled with tahini) 91

Shawarma, beef

Sandwichét Shawarma Lahmé (Beef shawarma with tarator & sumac téblé salad) 164

Shawarma, chicken

Sandwichét Shawarma Djej (Spiced chicken shawarma with fries, pickles & toum) 167

Spatchcock chicken

Farrouj Meshwé (Charcoal-grilled spatchcock chicken with toum & fries) 150

Spinach

Fatayer b'Sbenegh (Golden pastry parcels with tangy spinach & onion filling) 95

Strawberry purée

Atayef b'Joz (Stuffed Lebanese pancakes with walnuts & cinnamon) 182

Sultanas, golden

Freekeh b'Lahmé (Smoky roasted green wheat with lamb, sultanas & toasted nuts) 110

Sumac

Za'atar blend (for Mana'eesh Za'atar - Baked wild thyme, sumac & sesame flatbread) 35
Mana'eesh Banadoura (Baked tomato, onion, sumac & olive oil flatbread) 41
Salatet Banadoura (Tomato and cucumber salad - served with Ma'aalé) 63
Batata w Beid (Pan-fried potatoes & eggs with olive oil & Baharat) 67
Baba Ghanouj (Smoky aubergine salad) 83
Fatayer b'Sbenegh (Golden pastry parcels with tangy spinach & onion filling) 95
Salatet Fattoush (Lebanon's signature salad: colourful vegetables, crisp khobez & bright sumac) 100
Kastaleta (Lamb chops grilled over hot coals, marinated in garlic, lemon & Baharat) 147
Lahmé Meshwiyé (Tender lamb skewers, flame-grilled the Lebanese way) 153
Samké Meshwiyé (Grilled fish with tarator & smoky aubergine salad) 154
Sandwichét Shawarma Lahmé (Beef shawarma with tarator & sumac téblé salad) 164
Sandwichét Shawarma Djej (Spiced chicken shawarma with fries, pickles & toum) 167
Sandwichét Beid w Sumac (Scrambled eggs with sumac & pomegranate molasses) 171
Sandwichét Kafta (With hummus, pickles & onion salad) 167

Swiss chard

Adass bil Hamod (Lemony green lentil & Swiss chard soup) 49
Sélée Mehshi (Stuffed chard leaves with rice, mince & lemony broth) 132

T

Tahini
Hummus b'Thini (The pride of Lebanon: silky-smooth, tahini-rich & bright with lemon) 80
Mtabbal Batenjen (Creamy, garlicky, smoky: the real Lebanese mtabbal) 88
Sélée Mehshi (Stuffed chard leaves with rice, mince & lemony broth) 132
Tarator (Not just 'tahini sauce') 202

Tarator (tahini sauce)
Ma'aalé (Lebanon's favourite fried vegetables with tarator & pomegranate) 63
Salatet Fattoush (Lebanon's signature salad: colourful vegetables, crisp khobez & bright sumac) 100
Samke Harra (Spiced baked fish with tarator, pine nuts & coriander) 117
Kafta Meshwiyé (Charcoal-grilled minced meat skewers with tarator & téblé salad) 149
Samké Meshwiyé (Grilled fish with tarator & smoky aubergine salad) 154
Sandwichét Shawarma Lahmé (Beef shawarma with tarator & sumac téblé salad) 164
Sandwichét Falafel (Crispy falafel, turnip pickles & tarator) 172
Tarator (Not just 'tahini sauce') 202

Téh'wijé (herb and spice blend)
Fraké Nayyé (Southern-style spiced lamb tartare) 53
Kibbet Banadoura (Juicy tomato kibbé from the south) 54
Kibbet Batata (Mashed potato kibbé with burghul, herbs & onions) 56

Tomatoes, fresh
Ful w Hummus (Creamy fava beans & chickpeas mashed with garlic, lemon & olive oil) 24
Beid w Banadoura (Lebanese-style eggs with fresh tomatoes & olive oil) 27
Mana'eesh Kishek (Baked fermented yoghurt & burghul flatbread) 36
Mana'eesh Jibneh (Baked halloumi & Akkawi cheese flatbread) 39
Mana'eesh Banadoura (Baked tomato, onion, sumac & olive oil flatbread) 41
Lahém b'Ajine (Golden baked flatbread with spiced minced lamb) 43
Kibbet Banadoura (Juicy tomato kibbé from the south of Lebanon) 54
Loubieh b Zeit (Flat green beans simmered in tomatoes, garlic & olive oil) 60
Ma'aalé (Lebanon's favourite fried vegetables with tarator & pomegranate) 63
Baba Ghanouj (Smoky aubergine salad) 83
Khadija's Tabbouleh (The beginning of every gathering: my mum's tabbouleh) 92
Salatet Fattoush (Lebanon's signature salad: colourful vegetables, crisp khobez & bright sumac) 100
Bemieh b'Lahmé (Slow-cooked baby okra & lamb stew) 113
Fasoulia b'Lahmé (A hearty pot of butter beans & lamb, slowly simmered for deep flavour) 118
Kafta b'Sayniyeh (Kafta, potato & tomato traybake) 121
Maghmour (Lebanon's moussaka: aubergine baked with chickpeas, tomato & olive oil) 122
Bazella b'Lahmé (Lebanese-style lamb, peas & carrots in hearty tomato sauce) 125
Sélée Mehshi (Stuffed chard leaves with rice, mince & lemony broth - for base layer) 132
Sheikh el Mehshi (Baked baby aubergines stuffed with spiced mince in rich tomato sauce) 135
Sandwichét Shawarma Lahmé (Beef shawarma with tarator & sumac téblé salad) 164
Sandwichét Ma'aalé (Fried cauliflower & aubergine sandwich with creamy mtabbal) 168
Sandwichét Beid w Sumac (Scrambled eggs with sumac & pomegranate molasses) 171
Sandwichét Falafel (Crispy falafel, turnip pickles & tarator) 172
Sandwichét Kafta (With hummus, pickles & onion salad) 176

Tomatoes, tinned
Maghmour (Lebanon's moussaka: aubergine baked with chickpeas, tomato & olive oil) 122

Turnip
Kabiss Léfét (Lebanese pickled turnips) 201

Turnip pickles
Sandwichét Hummus (Street-style creamy hummus sandwich) 163
Sandwichét Shawarma Lahmé (Beef shawarma with tarator & sumac téblé salad) 164
Sandwichét Falafel (Crispy falafel, turnip pickles & tarator) 172

V

Vermicelli noodles
Shorbet Djej with Vermicelli (Soothing Lebanese chicken & vermicelli soup) 46
Réz m'Falfal (Lebanese rice with vermicelli) 126
Mloukhieh (Earthy jute mallow with tender chicken in a fragrant broth) 131

W

Walnuts
Lebanese Muhammara (Smoky roasted red pepper, walnut & olive oil dip) 86
Salatet Shamandar (Sweet, salty, crunchy beetroot, feta & walnut salad) 96
Samke Harra (Spiced baked fish with tarator, pine nuts & coriander) 117
Atayef b'Joz (Stuffed Lebanese pancakes with walnuts & cinnamon) 182

Watermelon, seedless
Salatet Halloum w Battikh (Grilled halloumi salad with watermelon, mint & olive oil) 71

Y

Yoghurt
Laban b'Khyar (Brown lentils & burghul with smoky onions: the pride of the South) 64
Labneh Mtawwameh (Garlicky labneh dip) 88
Shish Taouk (Classic Lebanese chicken skewers, grilled to smoky perfection) 158
Atayef b'Joz (Stuffed Lebanese pancakes with walnuts & cinnamon) 182
Nammoura (Sticky semolina cake with macerated plums) 186

Z

Za'atar (wild thyme/za'atar blend)
Mana'eesh Za'atar (Baked wild thyme, sumac & sesame flatbread) 35
Labneh Mtawwameh (Garlicky labneh dip) 88

Za'atar, leaves
Mana'eesh Jibneh (Baked halloumi & Akkawi cheese flatbread) 39
Zeitoun Mchakkal (Lebanese marinated green & black olives) 106

Acknowledgements

This book is more than just recipes – it's a piece of my life, my memories, and the people who shaped every part of them.

First and always, to my parents. To my mum – my forever mentor in the kitchen and in life. Everything I know about flavour, balance, and generosity started with you. I still call you to ask about a recipe (and yes, sometimes you still laugh and say, "You're the chef, not me!").

To my late father – your strength, discipline, and resilience taught me how to face life, push forward, and never give up. You built me solid, and for that I'm endlessly grateful.

To all my family in Lebanon and everywhere – my brothers, sisters, nieces and nephews – I'm the youngest, so you've all helped raise me one way or another!

To Aga, my partner in life and the real reason this book exists – without your endless support, patience, and belief, I wouldn't have written a single page. You've seen the chaos behind the calm, the late nights, and the endless tweaking of recipes. Thank you for standing beside me always. To my children, who joined me during shoots, tasted everything, and filled the days with joy (and plenty of cheeky comments) – you made this journey even more special.

To my incredible team at Lebnani, who keep the fire burning every single day, and to our loyal guests in Reigate and across Surrey – you've become family. You've shared our food, our story, and our dream.

To our amazing friends and collaborators, Melissa Thompson, Patricia Niven, Angela Clutton – your support, advice, and belief since day one has meant the world.

To my publisher Meze, and everyone who helped bring this dream to life – thank you.

To the most talented photographer Matt Russell, your eye captured the honesty and beauty of every dish, but it was the laughter, the music, and the endless jokes during those long shoot days that made it unforgettable.

To Tabitha Hawkins, the legend of prop styling – you understood exactly what I had in mind and gave every scene soul and beauty. Your energy lifted everyone's spirits.

To Ellie Mulligan, calm, precise, and beautifully collected – your quiet focus balanced my full-blown chef chaos perfectly. We made a great team.

To Katie Fisher, my editor, and Patrick Budge, my designer, thank you for turning my messy notes into something that looks this good.

To my suppliers, my trusted local butchers Robert & Edward, my fresh fruit and veg heroes at Fresh Connect, and all our Lebanese suppliers who keep the true taste of home alive in the UK.

To everyone who picks up this book, cooks from it, and shares it with loved ones, thank you. I hope you'll feel the warmth, the laughter, and the heart that went into every recipe.

And finally, the biggest thank you to everyone who supported our Kickstarter and made this project happen – you didn't just back a book, you backed a dream. I'll never forget this.

With love, gratitude, and a little bit of Lebanese chaos.

Shukran,

Jad

To those whose reward included this special thank you, your names are now part of our story, but every backer is forever part of the journey that made this cookbook possible.

Rachel Canham, Alex Maddox, Richard Norman, Elie Maamari, Angela Zaher, Florencia Tossutti, Mohammed El Bachouti, Annie-Marie Brigg, Rhiannon Ford, Nigel Kent, Julie Crossan, Annette Smith, Jamie Berry, Toby Brampton, Ann Horne, Chris Holden, Jonathan Parker, Tracy Musgrove, John Guy, Simon Slater, Melanie Hall, Hesham Shaban, Andrew Marsh, Sam Franco, James Tanser, Paul Allen, Ian Helmore, William Kieffer, Allen Stidwill, Rupert Yardley

Beirut days — the souk, the river,
and a bowl of fresh broad beans.